An Intelligent Person's Guide to History

An Intelligent Person's Guide to History

JOHN VINCENT

Professor of History
in the
University of Bristol

Duckworth

Revised and expanded edition 1996
First published in 1995 by
Gerald Duckworth & Co. Ltd.
The Old Piano Factory
48 Hoxton Square, London N1 6PB
Tel: 0171 729 5986
Fax: 0171 729 0015

A catalogue record for this book is available
from the British Library

ISBN 0 7156 2750 3

Typeset by Ray Davies
Printed and bound in Great Britain by
Biddles Ltd, Guildford and King's Lynn

Contents

I

History and Evidence

History is about evidence. It is also about other things: hunches, imagination, interpretation, guesswork. First and foremost, though, comes evidence: no evidence, no history.

It is about surviving evidence. Evidence that does not survive is no use, however plentiful it may once have been. It is also about intrinsically fallible evidence. In this it resembles medicine and the detection of crime. And it is about fallible evidence as interpreted by fallible people; hence no question of finality can ever arise.

Historical study requires verbal evidence, with marginal exceptions. And this verbal evidence, with all respect to the fascination of oral history, is nearly all written evidence. Writing is a broad term and includes the study of coins (numismatics) and epigraphy (the study of inscriptions), on which much of ancient history depends. But, however broadly interpreted, no writing normally means no history. Past speech, for instance, is normally unknowable; a huge distortion, but one intrinsic to history.

Studying the past is not possible: it is no longer there. All that can be studied are particular pieces of evidence, created in the first place usually for entirely non-historical reasons, which happen to survive into the present. Their survival, again, usually reflects accident, whether accident at the time of creation, or accident in the process of preservation and survival or both.

Nobody, or hardly anyone, created evidence for the convenience of future historians. Had they done so, it would be highly suspect. What ulterior purpose led them to try to influence the future? The Four Gospels convince because they are so full of discrepancies, so evidently not an attempt to impose a coherent historical record for all time.

Those in the present can only study evidence which exists in the present. That evidence is an infinitesimal part of the evidence which once existed. And there is a further obvious limitation. History is about literate societies, and strongly tilted, at very least, towards literate people in literate societies. As such, it is not the study of man; it is the study of the last five minutes on the human clock. Since active literacy has always been the exception, history can only speak directly of minorities. It is, at least until very recently, the study of stable, hierarchical, agricultural, aristo-cratic, and religious societies which create and preserve written evidence.

History is not, in practice, or in any simple sense, the study of mankind. It is the study, using some but not all methods, of some men in some societies at some times. It is the study, especially, of societies which preserve records and maintain continuity through long-lived institutions. Stone buildings help enormously; not all societies have stone buildings where paper can be kept safely down the centuries. History, or historical evidence, turns in the end on some very simple physical questions. The Great Fire of London did not, as it happened, destroy the immense records of the English medieval monarchy; but had it done so, or had the records been housed a mile nearer the flames, the study of medieval history as it has developed in the last century would be unrecognizably different.

Here let us pause briefly. History is a slippery word to use. It has two meanings. One is the study of the past, which is a human activity. The other meaning is the past itself, meaning an expanse of time. A human activity and an expanse of time are not remotely comparable – a case of chalk and cheese – yet we use the same word for both. This does not make life any easier. When Henry Ford said, 'History is bunk', did he mean that historical study is bunk, or that the past is bunk? Perhaps he meant both. Perhaps he forgot that today is tomorrow's historical past: singling out today as if it were a specially valuable field of study is hardly taking the long view. There is no parochialism like the parochialism of the present.

Back to this slippery word history. The theory of history, by the same token, has two meanings. One is theories about what the past was like, about whether there is some key to the past, some underlying rhythm: as Marx saw class struggle as underlying all history. The other sense of the theory of history is the theory of how one studies the past, of how history should be written, of historical method. Again, it is a case of chalk and cheese.

There is another word to fit in: historiography. In itself, it is not difficult. Coming from a Greek root (as in graphology) it means the writing of history, which is simple enough. Where some minds begin to spin, however, is when one comes to the history of historiography. This sounds more of a mouthful than it is: the history of historical study and historical writing is not intrinsically different from the history of anything else. In fact, in common practice the cumbrous term 'history of historiography' is usually abridged to 'historiography' pure and simple: an anomaly but a harmless one. Thus the 'historiography' of an issue will ordinarily mean the history of the development of the views expressed by successive historians of that question.

Only the most alert avoid sometimes confusing the two meanings of history, and this book, relying on the intelligence of its readers and upon context, will not even try.

That parenthesis behind us, back to our main theme of history and evidence, this time with examples. Things can be defined in two ways: what they are, and what they are not. There are some things which history certainly is not. It is not a study of the non-human past. Such subjects as glaciology, dendrochronology, astronomy, geology, palaeontology, subjects which can deal with a past far more distant than any known to historians, are not history. Some of these, like dendrochronology, the study of tree rings, interact with history, since the oldest trees go back to 4000 BC, and the annual variations in their growth provide a structure for dating. But on the whole, the study of the past by means of science has little to do with history.

History is not about pre-literate societies. It has little to say about hunting, nomadic, pastoral, or gathering people, except in so far as they were observed from outside. (The cowboy Wild West survives through its impact on the imaginations of settled societies.) Even if a horseman of the steppes could write, where could

he preserve his writing for future generations? Absence of records
is nothing to do with importance or power: the great invading
hordes from central Asia, such as the Huns and Tartars, did not
lack power. But records they did lack – unless and until they
conquered a civilisation of cities, bureaucracies and great estates
and adopted its ways.

There is a persuasive but unsound version of history which
ignores this dividing line between the written and unwritten. It is
a version often first encountered in early days at primary school,
and vividly retained. It looks back to 10,000 BC, to the end of the
Ice Age. It draws on a mixture of surmise, on an increasingly
long archaeological record in the Middle East, and on the pictur-
esque. It is history as seen in museums. It implants a valuable
sense of human continuities since the Ice Age which puts the
period of recorded history in truer perspective. It implants, too,
a sense of inexorable material progress, and of the speeding-up
of history as the present approaches. But, for all its merits, the
elementary story of early man, particularly if made coherent, is
not so much history as the context in which history may, or may
not, have occurred. It is also a golden dream of a world unmud-
died by beliefs, events, intentions, thoughts, follies, all creatures
of written testimony. Early, pre-literate man, unlike us, makes
no mistakes, and cannot be wrong. There lies the greatest discontinuity between the accidentally pre-literate and the
accidentally literate epochs.

History is not archaeology, for the very good reason that properly speaking the latter is a method not a body of knowledge.
Unlike history, it is focused on material objects not thoughts. In
theory, and often in practice, it is applicable to any society or
period. It is only colloquially that archaeology has come to apply
specifically to pre-literate societies or to prehistory. Archaeology,
being a method, can be, and is, used to study literate medieval
societies, or even advanced societies, as in the case of industrial
archaeology with its loving resurrection of rusty steam engines
and Victorian factories.

Should the historian have roots in prehistory? Emphatically,
yes: deep ones, for prehistory is only history minus an alphabet,
and the infancy of society was marked by many changes far more

salient than the arrival of writing – consider for instance the domestication of wild animals, the invention of textiles, or some wholly unrecorded great event like the Indo-European cultural expansion throughout most of Eurasia, the greatest of political events, comparable only to the universal spread of firearms. The gap between prehistory and history is a gap in our methods of study, not a gap in what went on in the past.

History is not just about evidence, or even about surviving evidence. To take another way of looking at it, it is either about too much evidence, or too little. Too much, first: we know, more or less exactly, the number of books printed in England. Between 1475, the beginning of English printing, and 1640, we have 36,000 titles; between 1641 and 1700, a further 100,000 titles appeared; in the eighteenth century a further 350,000 titles appeared, including all works printed in English anywhere, and all works in a foreign language printed in the British Empire. In short, for the modern or early modern historian, evidence, at least for some things, is superabundant. (How long does it take to read and analyse a single book?) And this superabundance takes into account only one type of evidence, books; the question of unprinted papers, letters, and diaries would raise just the same sense of surfeit, albeit one not so readily quantified.

There is, about modern times, just too much evidence; and contrarily about ancient times there is just too little evidence. To have the right amount of evidence, no more, no less, is by far the least likely possibility. The past did not arrange matters to suit present needs – why should it have? And even if the evidence were just right, just what we were looking for, that in itself should make one smell a rat, for nothing can be more suspect than evidence that is just right. The question of overabundance and its reverse is, to put it mildly, something of a difficulty.

One extreme case concerns human nature itself. Here history – the past – is an experiment that was cut short just as it was getting interesting. One can draw no conclusions about what man would be like if different localities had been left to go their own way, because the process of global convergence in the last four centuries has stopped the experiment. Thus the Incas were cut short in 1530 after only a century; the Aztecs after a shorter ascendancy. History has to make do with but two great written traditions, the Eurasian and the East Asian, a trifle in relation to all the communities that have existed, and the still larger number that would have existed but for Eurasian expansion. On such small evidence, no judgment can be reached as to man's potential variousness, or lack of it. History is a badly designed experiment.

Consider two other extreme cases where the historian does not have what he wants, but what he gets. First, the ancient world. The Roman Empire was a large affair, a huge, literate, rationally administered, urbanized fact, extending over at least six centuries. From it there survive ten million words in Latin, and 100 million in Greek. Of these, 90% in each case are post-Christian. Had it been pagans who decided what survived from antiquity, the proportion of Christian and non-Christian material might have looked very different.

Of the ten million words in Latin, two million concern Roman law, because lawyers found them worth preserving. Only one million are pre-Christian. Of the ten million words of pre-Christian Greek, two million are by the medical writer 'Galen'. To survive the Dark Ages, it was advisable to stick to writing legal or medical works, and to be a Christian. The remote past has already censored the remoter past.

The remote past has already determined even the form and shape of what survives. The Bible may be a divine book. But that it is a book at all, arises from the invention about 200 AD of books in place of scrolls. Instead of a heap of papyrus scrolls, it was physically possible to have a single book that one could call the New Testament. The available technology of the day marked out the limits of literary possibility.

In our own time, the technical basis of history has changed beyond recognition. For four centuries, the nature of evidence had remained remarkably stable: letters, letters, letters. (The monastic chronicle vanished with the dissolution of the monasteries.) Then the mirror shivers and cracks. Letters became telephone calls; conversation there had always been, but putting conversation on paper was no longer necessary. Evidence, of a new kind, was increased by the use of the tape recorder in oral history, a technique first adopted in the U.S.A. in 1948. The power to create non-contemporaneous evidence increased, as the power to check it against contemporary evidence diminished. (The difficulty with oral history is not that old men forget, but that they remember with startling clarity what they wrote, misleadingly, long ago.)

The twentieth-century state generates paper as never before. It then destroys it as never before. The United Kingdom produces about 100 miles of government records each year, of which only one mile is kept. We destroy, not to hide the truth, but because we lack room. Again, the crudely physical element predominates.

Hiding the truth nevertheless has come to matter more. In the 1960s, responding to the cry of 'More Openness', Harold Wilson's government changed the Fifty-Year Rule governing access to official papers, to a thirty-year rule. Now a difference of twenty years may not seem much, but to those in high places it meant that all they wrote would probably come before public scrutiny during their lifetime, and very possibly during their active career. In those circumstances, what is called 'writing for the dossier' is bound to occur on a large scale. The disparity between evidence and reality, always there even when it was not expected that letters would be seen by others, has become an abyss. To those who like to think that they know what went on, the Thirty-Year Rule was a great step forward; to those who want to know what really went on, it was a disaster. Records, like compost, are best well rotted.

Men write letters because they are apart. So long as the holders of power lived in country houses, or on great estates, they had of necessity to write to their own kind. When in the capital, as for the London political and social season, there was less reason to write, for they met daily anyway. For considered correspondence, one may well find that the long period of rusticity between mid-August and late January, when parliament did not sit and hardly a dog barked, evoked more political evidence than the busy months of spring and summer. In a world of country houses, the volume, frequency, and depth of letters may be in inverse ratio to the seriousness of events.

That is a world we have lost. We can no longer write 'normal' history, because we no longer have that kind of society. Whether there can be history under late twentieth-century electronic conditions, remains to be seen, but the only safe assumption is that it will bear little resemblance to post-Renaissance historical study, above all where individual motive is concerned. A study based on the written word cannot survive the marginalization of paper. We may be on the verge of a new prehistory, with the era of serious, intricate, intimate knowledge of the past merely a fortunate interlude. Electronic communication means no history. The fashion for open access means no history. The mass production of evidence, and its mass destruction on an equally industrialized scale, means no history. Unrecorded history means no history, or at least, as in prehistory, a history of material matters at the expense of thought.

History is about primary sources. All secondary sources were primary sources once, even if the originals no longer survive. Indeed, a primary source is a secondary source which has not yet been interpreted. All primary sources are suspect; their destiny is to add to misunderstanding. When the great archives of Venice were opened in the early nineteenth century, the classic opening of a Pandora's box which offered to tell all, it took time and reflection to discern that ambassadors' reports tell us as much about the ambassador, as about the country discussed, and that the most wily Venetian, precisely because he was a wily Venetian, would see so alien an institution as the Elizabethan parliament with perplexed and unseeing eyes.

Primary sources are never innocent, never above temptation, never undeserving of a sceptical eye. No eye-witness ever stands up to comparison with another eye-witness of the same event. (The essential quality of a reliable eye-witness account is that there should be no other eye-witnesses.) Yet, when compared to memoirs – admittedly not a demanding comparison – those primary sources written in the belief that nobody except the recipient will ever see them, do perhaps enjoy a certain extra credibility. In this category fall most of the diplomatic correspondence and political letters on which so much post-Renaissance history depends. Even these, however private and secret, cannot be viewed as plain statements of fact. They represent attempts to influence, to persuade, to impress, to convince, to manipulate. They are not neutral. And diaries? They may have been written for nobody but the writer. This one rarely knows; and such chastity of motive is not supported by the fact of their preservation. Still, a writer, whether of diaries or letters, who believes that he will never be caught out, has all the greater temptation to deceive, not by plain lying, but by putting a good face on his part in things.

Progress in historical studies in the last two centuries has relied heavily on using unprinted archival primary sources. Archives were seen as a means of grace. This approach became 'the thing to do'. School exams mimed it, university promotions depended upon it. Gibbon, who used primary sources, but ones printed by predecessors, came to seem an armchair historian, a model of what not to be. The cult of the primary source became equated with the cult of the manuscript archive. After all, the wish to discover a secret is a powerful motive. Yet, as A.J.P. Taylor said, all the secrets are already in print.

This is true at least in that there is an imbalance in status and esteem between archival sources, whose drawbacks are less readily grasped than their positive qualities, and *The Times*, Hansard, and the books of the period. One point is of practical value: that *The Times* and Hansard, being meticulously indexed, are the past at its most accessible. Butterfield said that it might take a hundred years for historians to regain the knowledge of the past that an intelligent newspaper reader had at the time. Intelligent reading of newspapers, and of Hansard, has been one of the weaker points of the historical revolution of the last two centuries. The search for hidden truth has led to a bias against print, perhaps even against books; print is the Venetian archive of tomorrow.

Perhaps this is the point at which to consider the three degrees of historical subtlety in accessing primary sources. The first stage is plain credulous unsubtlety: believing the evidence. This means believing what people say about themselves, believing statements of principle, political speeches, what you read in the newspapers, and believing what the police or their historical predecessors say in court, on oath or elsewhere. This was often not so naive as it may sound. In a world of gentlemen, where a reputation for sharp practice was counter-productive, taking a gentlemen's word as truth was natural, in its way fairly sensible, and in itself served to raise expectations for the better.

The second degree of subtlety went to the other extreme of

disbelief: disbelieving the newspapers, the police, the politicians, disbelieving what people say about themselves (with the lingering exception of Mr Gladstone), disbelieving above all statements of principle. This view of things will always be associated with the great work of Sir Lewis Namier in the 1920s. In essence, he said, or was held to have said, that political men were creatures of ambition or habit, that principle was the figleaf of the political operator, and that slogans were consequences, not causes, of the animal pushing and shoving of politics.

The third degree of subtlety rejects this view as doctrinaire, narrow, above all unsubtle. To those on these giddy heights, all evidence is evidence; there is no such thing as evidence which is not admissible. All evidence tells us something, is a symptom of something, is not to be brushed aside. Every slogan is a fact. A political speech may be outright charlatanism from start to finish, but putting contents aside, its timing, its rhetoric, its choice of audience, may be crucial bits of the jigsaw; and since there are many versions of charlatanism, it is important that one version was chosen rather than another. Omissions, too, are evidence, as much as the most palpable fact: what a speech or a letter omits to say, may be the most important fact about it. Silence is evidence.

Every dog has its day. In the world in which modern historical scholarship grew up, the prestige of documents bore all before it. It was documents that made or unmade historians' careers; documents, where the ultimate secrets were thought to lie. Documents have had a good run over the last two centuries; but these centuries may be untypical. Today, the place to look for secrets is, for British historians, in the press. This is *terra incognita*, and in the case of the press, with good reason. Only in one library, the Newspaper Library of the British Library, in the rather remote north London suburb of Colindale, Hendon, can one consult a wide run of national and local papers. Otherwise, libraries hold *The Times* and perhaps a few others, but writing history from *The Times*, and especially writing the history of opinion, is necessarily precarious. As always, practice has determined principle, and the principle of the primacy of the truly 'authentic' unprinted source arises, at least in modern British history, quite largely from very ordinary considerations of practicability. Hendon is far, its newspaper holdings voluminous, and life is short.

History is incorrigibly male, though much less so than it was. That is not to say that it will remain so in the future, still less that it should. It is not to say that women mattered, or matter, less than men, whatever such a statement might mean. It does not deny that the body of evidence relating to women is large, depending on time and place. It does not deny the huge recent expansion in the amount of historical writing about women.

It means one thing only: that women have characteristically created less evidence, so obviously so that argument upon the point is idle. It may mean that women had better things to do than live their lives on paper. At any rate, the past is incorrigibly male, as it is incorrigibly aristocratic, incorrigibly religious, incorrigibly unfair. To those who object, there can be only one answer. Things are as they are, and not as we would have them be.

That women play men's roles only adds to the difficulty of assessing the place of women in history. When a woman does heavy manual labour, or succeeds without obvious effort on her part through male rules to a crown or other high position, there is nothing specifically female about her role. The question of heiresses is important: throughout history, the great majority of prominent women were so not because they had the talents of a Virginia Woolf, the will of a Florence Nightingale, or the inspiration of a Joan of Arc, but for no better reason than that their father had died, leaving them without brothers. If it is not so today, it is because the comtemporary world is very unlike that of history, perhaps nowhere more so than in the case of women. In the deep past, however, the most prominent individual women, and many of those creating evidence, have often been, and perhaps had to be, honorary males (males mediate conflict, women know better). Here complexity rules: Queen Victoria, wife, mother, widow, and untutored miss, not to say voluminous diarist, left evidence galore of deep femininity, probably more so than her fellow-ruler Elizabeth I. But as the latter name suggests, women do play male roles under male rules, do step into male shoes, and this complicates any assessment. Again, things are as they are, and not as we (or modern feminism) would have them be; it is a bit late to set about remodelling the past in accordance with modern standards.

History is not about youth. History is incorrigibly about the relatively old. The average historical individual, if one can imagine such a person, is probably about 50, an age at which ardours have cooled and most are satisfied enough to be what they are, and to take things as they find them. Here then we find the great divide between literature and history: literature is about being under 30, or under 40, as one may choose. History will then take over, and do a far better job at saying what being over 40 is like. This is arbitrary, for all will recall King Lear and Prospero. But youth, as a condition to be borne, is not a topic that history can do much to explore. On individual emotion, at least outside the public domain, history speaks with a quavering and uncertain voice. In history, boy does not meet girl; that is, there is a whole side of life whose deepest truths are to be found in the realm of imaginative litera-ture, and these truths are on the whole the truths of youth. History picks up where literature leaves off, and that means with the relatively old.

History is about winners, not losers. In broad terms, this is because the winners write the history. In narrow terms, it is because those risking the gallows would have been foolish to damn themselves on paper. Thus the private papers of the Chartists were scanty, while for their middle-class contemporaries, the Anti-Corn Law League, an almost daily epistolary record of their inner thoughts survives. The reason? The Chartists faced prison, the League did not; though lack of offices and business habits played a part.

Again, in Thomas Pakenham's *The Year of Liberty*, on the great 1798 uprising in Ireland, he writes of finding 10,000 documents on the government side, filed under the heading 'Rebellion Papers', but of tracing only 100 surviving rebel documents. In such cases, history has to be told as experienced by the government and their informants, irrespective of where one's own sympathies may lie.

Another loser, of a very different kind, has been the Labour Party in modern British history, and it is especially Labour minis-ters of the first two or three generations whose papers are missing. Their houses were small, at least by Conservative standards, and their widows wanted the space. Even regarding recent records, the authors of *British Cabinet Ministers 1900-1951*, writing while the trail was still hot, reported that 'We have tried to find the papers of 323 Cabinet Ministers. In 73 cases loss or destruction of the collections seem certain.'

Some losers remain forever in our mind: Joan of Arc, Cranmer. That is because they were losers who won. But the picture we hold is a picture created by hostile authorities. It is the person as seen by the authorities who endures, not the person as they really were. It is the authorities who create, handle, and preserve the evidence, above all in state trials or police records. Yet Cranmer, the humble archbishop burnt at the stake with all he had lived for in ruin, is the classic case of the loser who was really incomparably victorious: his liturgy, the Book of Common Prayer, shaped the English mind for four centuries, united Englishmen as nothing else did, and reached a world Shakespeare never touched. So the distinction between winners and losers may be far from simple.

Wandering into parenthesis for a moment, consider the curious case of that universal figure, the conscientious magistrate. He may be conscientious, but perhaps a little ambitious too; he certainly wants to stand well with the central authorities, whose only local representative he is, and he is not immune from temptation. His letters to London, or Paris, or Madrid, will therefore err on the alarmist side. He will speak of great dangers, knowing that he cannot lose. If the dangers do not take place, that speaks well for his zeal, his control of the situation; if things go badly wrong, he will at least be on record as having given due warning, and no one will be able to impugn his foresight. The man on the spot (be he magistrate, diplomatist, or soldier) precisely because he is on the spot, is subject to his very own special temptation, perhaps unconscious or habitual. The paradox of the conscientious magistrate should ever be in our mind when we talk of the value of primary sources.

History is about evidence, but only about evidence we approve of. Evidence we disapprove of, might as well not exist. We decide, even before looking at it, what can be evidence and what not. Thus with miracles; thus with witchcraft.

The body of evidence in favour of miracles could not be of higher quality. It is based on the testimony of eye-witnesses. It is contemporaneous. It is massive in bulk. It comes from educated men. It is often entirely disinterested. It varies little over a large number of centuries. There is little evidence contrary to the idea of special providences, and perhaps there could not be. The historical evidence for miraculous intervention could not be weightier. Our decision to disregard it is not a historical decision, not an induction from the evidence as it is. It is based on our non-historical or *a priori* belief (for belief it is) that there is no such thing as the miraculous.

The same with witchcraft. For two centuries the best minds gave it credence: Shakespeare, for instance. By what right do we look to him as on the one hand a source of profoundest truth, and on the other a man who swallowed, perhaps propagated, the most transparent of fallacies? The evidence for witchcraft is in some ways of even higher standing than that for miracles. For it is sworn evidence, evidence given in court, fully and instantaneously recorded, a matter of due process of law, evidence very widely accepted not just by popular opinion but by the official mind. It is thus evidence, however wrongly obtained or subject to ulterior motive, which does not differ in form from that given in other legal cases of the period.

If we disbelieve in witchcraft, it is despite the evidence. History is about evidence, but we decide, or the general culture of our day decides, what to exclude from evidence. It is not lack of evidence, but a general antecedent belief that such things ought to be untrue, with which adherents of the existence of UFOs and the Bermuda Triangle vainly contend. Evidence means evidence we approve of.

History is about evidence. History as art, just as much as history as science, has to respect its constraints. History is inescapably tied to the written word. Where the written word stops, there history stops and geography, probably, begins. Landscape and architecture, though important as sources, need the survival of past words to give them meaning. (Hence the mystery of the Sphinx.) History excludes important non-literate civilizations and includes unimportant literate ones. History is not the story of man, even of post-Ice Age man. The difference between record-preserving societies and non-record-preserving societies can sometimes be

marginal. History is climatic: evidence prefers very wet surround-
ings, as in the Northumbrian peat bogs which preserve Roman
soldiers' letters, or very dry ones, as with the papyri of the Egyp-
tian desert. History needs stone buildings, stable aristocracies,
enduring bureaucracies. Almost everywhere, historical evidence is
and has always been physically insecure.

History is deeply male. History is essentially non-young. History is about the rich and famous, not the poor. History favours
the articulate, not the silent. History is about winners (including
those losers who were eventual winners), not about losers. History is about assessing distortions, not copying out truths.
History has to live with, is indeed the child of censorship: the
censorship by one culture of its predecessor, the censorship by a
great modern bureaucracy of its own overproduction of records,
the censorship of astute reticence by those aware that the eye of
posterity will watch them. History has much to say about the
way the powerful handle power, for power engenders records.
History is almost silent (so far) on psychology, but copious on
sociology in the sense of social structure (less so, perhaps, on
sociology as values). History is hopeless on love, but excellent on
hatred. Such a state of things may not please all, but then it was
never meant to please. One-sidedness lies at the heart of historical knowledge.

History is about arranging bits of paper. History, or historical
writing, is therefore difficult but not hard. Its constraints are not
ones which intelligence can remove. The highest mental powers,
those of a Bach or a Newton, are not required, because even the
loftiest intellect is as much at a loss as one of common clay in
apprehending what is not knowable. The studies of psychologists
suggest that a very modest I.Q. will suffice to make a successful
historian, if motivation and curiosity are there (and one might
surely add physical stamina, and a certain indifference to bore-
dom). To relate men to their context, the essential historical skill,
is an everyday kind of activity, even if for the historian it involves
a slightly obsessional concern with paper, another trait on which
psychologists have had their say. It is a central paradox of historical study that the exploration of human feeling in all its
magnificence has to be done by scholarly moles and meticulous

mice who, however rollicking when off duty, must professionally be bureaucratic arrangers of information.

II

History and Meaning:
What Meaning Means

Beyond evidence, lies meaning.

An example. Consider an Englishman and American watching a cricket match, in all its arcane ritual. Both see exactly the same phenomena. Both are eye-witnesses of events. In terms of evidence, they are on an equal footing. But one, the Englishman, understands the meaning of what is going on, while the American finds it incomprehensible.

Evidence, then, without meaning, is nothing. And historians have to bring their meaning to the evidence: empiricism is not enough. The American, left to himself, will not grasp what cricket is about just by being an onlooker.

He will, of course, see that after six balls, the players changed ends. This is an empirical historical fact. It describes, but does not explain. It leaves intention rather in the dark. It is chronicle, as opposed to history.

The American, without any prior knowledge, may continue his observations, leading him to remark that bowling six balls makes them change ends, except, he will prudently add, when they do not, as at the end of an innings. Here he moves from observation to generalization, as does the historian when he says that poll taxes cause peasants' revolts, or that divided parties lose elections, adding, of course, as a scientist would hardly do, except when they do not do so.

The American has perhaps gone as far as he can, and the cricketing analogy becomes tiresome. But there is this: the Englishman knows the meaning of what is going on, knows it in terms of intention, and the habitual acceptance of conventions making up a game, and what matters or is notable, and what not. Yet both Englishman and American see the same phenomena. Seeing, and understanding the meaning, are worlds apart.

There are enough disagreements to consider among historians about the nature of their subject, without diverging far into the difference between historical study and science. Two questions arise: is history a science or an art? If a science, does it resemble natural science?

It does not resemble natural science, as is easily shown; or, to play safe, most forms of historical study do not resemble most forms of traditional natural science. History concerns motives: science does not. Atoms do not have motives; people do. Science gives the same results in every place and time; history is incapable of such replication, for each historical event is unique. History is not concerned with seeking underlying laws, as much of physical science does (or perhaps did). History is not much concerned with the type or the average: even in biological science, when dissecting a frog, one's concern is with features common to all frogs, rather than the ways in which one particular frog is unique. And in history, unlike in science, one cannot use control groups to test a hypothesis; or at very least, it would be difficult, and uncommon, to do so.

The points made above constitute a standard answer, and one which nine out of ten historians would probably accept. History is not a science, if by science one means traditional ideas of physical science. Perhaps this is a question of verbal usage, for in English the word science marks a sharp division, whereas the German counterpart *Wissenschaft* denotes the underlying unity of all thought and learning. Thus, if our verbal usage was more like the German, we might end by arguing that history was both science (in its own way) and art. For all that, putting mere verbal nuance aside, we would still have to stress in how many ways history is very unlike most of the natural sciences.

Historians try not only to describe the past; they try to explain it. Only very rarely does the past supply any explanation of itself. The attempt to supply the meaning of the past is the distinguishing feature of history (as it is, in principle, of social science in its broadest sense). The presence of meaning, rather than the absence of laws, is the distinction that matters most: meaning involving thought, motive, intention, and lack of intention, things with which science has obviously no business.

The presence, or absence, of laws and predictable regularities is a distinction on which too much has been made to rest in the past. It will ever remain a fair point; but science is itself various and shifting, and to an outsider, particle physics sometimes seems to resemble the more wildly intuitive forms of history. Some forms of science need laws, others less so. The issue is not the universality of laws within all sciences, but that where science asserts, say, the Second Law of Thermodynamics, it is asserting something more than a pattern with inevitable exceptions.

Historians do deal in patterns: at least, some do, and some do not. But even those who do not, would not object in principle to it being said that medieval monarchies wane through the progressive alienation of territory to overmighty subjects – a common enough pattern – provided that there is always the whispered qualification 'except when it is different'. However faithfully traced a historical pattern may be, there is never certainty that next time the pattern will repeat itself. Thus patterns are not laws.

History does not resemble natural science. As shown above, there are up to five big differences, though of varying weight. There may be a sixth difference. It is about the place of authority in science considered as an educational subject. There is little room for difference of opinion, or opinion at all, in anatomy, chemistry, or physics. One cannot reinterpret the breastbone, or take a novel view of sulphuric acid, at least while climbing the educational ladder. While the steps to scientific truth may rest on re-treading the ladder of reasoning, the ultimate result rests on authority: this is the truth, this is the right answer, this is what authority says one must think. So a scientific education, for all its laudable culture of reason and experiment, is for most of those experiencing it, mildly but necessarily authoritarian, because authoritative.

History is anarchic, not authoritarian. A freshman may trump a professor, not in knowledge, but in interpretation. Even an examination answer may show a quite new insight. History knows no last word on any subject. The bigger and better-trodden the subject – for instance the origins of the First World War – the more often it can be reinterpreted. This is because history is not about learning, or learnedness, but about meaning, in whose domain authority has little sway.

But, it may be said, the Norman Conquest after all certainly took place in 1066. The Normans won at Hastings, and that is that. The answer is robust – that is very much not that. One man may think that the Normans won; another that they lost, disastrously, all that mattered – all hope of being more than a subordinate polity ruled from London, and that defeat on that day alone could have saved them from the slippery slope that led to the absorption, sooner rather than later, of Normandy into France. The differences in interpretation far outweigh in fullness of meaning any agreement on the observed phenomena. Certainly, no appeal to authority can settle such debates; seeing the same event does not entail agreement on its meaning, for the sense of its meaning is supplied in an almost fictional way from the historian's inner nature.

The historian understands, the scientist reasons. Historical study is not an act of scientific reasoning; but if not that, what else? The something else, various philosophers of historical thought have said, must be an act of imagination, or imaginative re-enactment. In saying this, philosophers like Croce in Italy, Dilthey in Germany, Collingwood and Winch in England, are not saying that historians are mere historical novelists, unconstrained by historical accuracy. No: they are saying that a pre-condition of accuracy, in any full sense, is re-thinking or re-imagining the thought of the past.

In a negative way, this makes good sense. Re-thinking the past in terms of present-day preoccupations is hindsight, the worst mistake a historian can make – a matter on which consensus runs broad and deep (and should therefore be questioned, as later it will be). Never forget that people in the past did not know what came next, any more than we do. The limits of human prediction can be measured in months rather than years. To share the past's understanding of itself, one must share its ignorance of what came next.

Still, some down to earth thoughts about this heady wine of

imagining past thought come quickly to mind. They are not necessarily fatal objections, but they are certainly objections. There are,
I think, not less than four commonsense difficulties.

First, of how many people in the present do you know their inner
thoughts? Any? Enough to write a coherent study of contemporary
society? Do you really know the deepest motives of your own
family? And if knowing the thought of another person is hard
enough in the present, how can we hope to apply it to those known
to us only on paper?

Secondly, we all conceal our intentions and feelings to some
extent, but leaders and persons of note have, by training, habit,
and necessity, worn masks of ambiguity and artificiality to such an
extent that speaking of an underlying reality is often almost
impossible. The public figure is so unlike the private figure that
imagining past thought by analogy with our own private thought
is a snare and delusion.

Thirdly, how does one verify the re-enactment of past thought,
that is, why is my re-enactment better than that of another person
(or are all equally good, on the principle of giving marks for effort?).

Fourthly, there is the fact that the philosophers of historical
imagination write not from pure love of truth, but with a certain
axe to grind. Their theories are not plucked from a blue sky, but
are a retort – a retort to the dominance and prestige of natural
science in the nineteenth century, and perhaps of a semi-scientific
social science in the twentieth century. Philosophies of historical
method were an attempt to meet pretension with pretension, and
cannot claim purity of motive.

So much for the cold water. For all that, there could be no
introduction to history which neglected its poetry. Meaning is the
poetry of history, evidence the prose. British academic historians,
if asked what their philosophy of history was, would probably
either return a dusty answer, or say that they thought Collingwood
was broadly right (except, they would cautiously add, where he
was wrong). Because he was a talented sloganizer, because he
wrote in English, because, being published in an early Penguin, he
caught the ear of the postwar generation, Collingwood is for practical purposes the most available philosopher of history (in the
sense of how one studies the past, not in the sense of how the past

works) that we have, despite some diminution of his stature by the advent of Marxism and social sciences in the Sixties.

Who was Collingwood, and why does he matter?

III

Historical Imagination:
Why Collingwood Matters

Everybody is for historical imagination. Explaining how it works is another matter. Explaining how, if at all, one verifies an imaginative act, is a task for heroes.

R.G. Collingwood (1889-1943), Professor of Philosophy at Oxford from 1935 to 1941, certainly did his best to provide a philosophy of historical method. He was in some ways well equipped to do so; in others not. He wrote widely on the philosophy of art, religion, metaphysics, even though his reputation rests mainly on his philosophy of history, which he thought his chief work. As a philosopher, he was deeply out of sympathy with the dominant school of his time, that of logical positivism, a dogmatic creed which murdered to dissect, but did not construct. 'The best-known neglected thinker of his time' was a description which conveyed the marginal position he held in his own generation.

Collingwood was also a leading authority on Roman Britain and Romano-British archaeology, and wrote the volume on Roman Britain in the Oxford History of England. Given his inevitable reliance on archaeological evidence, he was very untypical of the normal historian working from books and papers, and the peculiar difficulties of writing about Roman Britain inform his philosophy of history, as set forth in his *Autobiography* (1939) and his posthumous *Idea of History*.

His success was based on the wide popularization of his ideas, his gift for embodying his ideas in lively slogans, his recognition of the essentially autonomous and non-scientific character of history (with all that that implied for the prestige and status of history as an activity in its own right rather than a pale shadow of science), and in his clothing a tradition of historical imagination going back to Sir Walter Scott in respectable philosophic clothes.

To Collingwood, his philosophy of history was a unity; to us, its components are best considered separately. There is his central assertion that 'all history is the history of thought'. From this it followed that history taught self-knowledge, and through self-knowledge, by a further reckless leap in the argument, it might become a school of political wisdom, operating upon the world of practical affairs. Thirdly, history was 'the science of human affairs', destined to equal the natural sciences. Fourthly, history was a matter of asking the right questions.

This last point, half exhortation, half truism, deserves easy assent. An answer cannot be better than its question. The discovery of good questions is half the battle; good questions lead to good answers. For teacher and student, this is something to ram home. Before pen touches paper, decide what questions one proposes to answer – a commonplace, but rarely done. There is a deceptive simplicity about all this, for if history is about asking good questions, the evidence will not in itself choose what the questions ought to be. As Collingwood put it, with his archaeological experience in mind, it is a question of getting away from 'let us dig and see what we can find' to knowing what problems you wish to solve: 'study problems, not sites'. Two men digging in the same trench would produce different answers, because they were asking different questions. Beneath the surface of this apt schoolroom homily, lies a riposte of rationalism against empiricism: rationalism, because it is the historian who constructs in his own mind the structures about which questions should be put. It is not simply by describing the scattered and arbitrary empirical phenomena that one establishes what one needs to know.

Next, what of Collingwood's high, indeed grandiose, and apparently arrogant view of the place of history? At first sight, his assertions are indeed extravagant. He saw us as 'standing on the threshold of an age in which history would be as important for the world as natural science had been between 1600 and 1900'. He believed that a revolution in historical thought in the twentieth century would parallel the scientific revolution of the seventeenth century. History was 'the newest and latest form of knowledge': no reticence here, and to us, with history now occupying no very special place in the world of education, it makes no sense unless rephrased to allow for context. In Collingwood's time, history was the dominant arts subject, the dominant social science too – with economics, English, modern languages very much in the wings, and classics a stately rearguard. To speak of historical study and to speak of the study of man, could, at that date and viewed from an Oxford window, appear all but synonymous. It is only when one substitutes 'social sciences' (including, institutional quirks apart, history) for Collingwood's 'history' that one begins to see the force of his claims. To anyone who has experienced the growth of the social sciences, however defined, since 1960, it must seem that in their speedy rise to authority, their lamentable self-sufficiency, their unabashed assertiveness, they really do constitute that challenge to natural science which Collingwood had in mind when he spoke of history.

Collingwood's next claim was that historical study led to self-knowledge, and self-knowledge made history a school of political wisdom (here he wrote, in the shadow of the Great War and the Third Reich, with a naive urgency that looks dated today). In a broad sense, his claims were almost true – except that he meant them in a narrow sense.

Historical study leads to broader views, to escape from the parochialism of the present, to an understanding that there were once other standpoints as commanding as the tenets of today. Perhaps there is a latitudinarianism implicit in history, and probably this works to the good, except of course when it does the reverse. For an instance of the latter, consider the pernicious theories of race, which normally rest on historical not biological foundations, or the fanaticism engendered or justified by Irish preoccupation with 'seven centuries of Saxon misrule'. History has a dark underside; Britain and America are lucky, and exceptional, in escaping the worst consequences of past obsessions, and so perhaps are inclined to overestimate the benefits of history. The English and American Civil Wars lead to no deaths today, but this is the exception not the rule.

The idea of history as a school of political wisdom went back to the Renaissance, and flourished in eighteenth- and nineteenth-century England. Its premise was essentially not intellectual, but sociological: the notion of bright and ambitious young men, of good birth, destined for public service and great responsibilities, coming at a formative age to all the past could teach. Even recently, such a vision tinged, but no more than tinged, Oxford and Cambridge; it may be that departments of economics are still sometimes nurseries of ambition, as is financial journalism. Departments of history, as nurseries of ordinariness, cannot justify themselves in this way. Whatever their justification, it is not the training of a political elite; an idea that in any case found it difficult to outlive the sharp decline in the predominance of strictly political history after 1960, as well as growing moral uncertainty about 'elitism'. (Perhaps strangely, the economic historians have been fairly reluctant to generalize about their speciality as a source of economic wisdom.)

Amidst such broad arguments, Collingwood's claims for history as leading to self-knowledge form a distinctly special case. Neither a broadening of view, nor a tutored political wisdom, are quite the same as self-knowledge, and indeed are not to be confused with it. Enhanced self-knowledge, as Collingwood saw it, was to be obtained by re-enacting the past thoughts of others (meaning, usually, individuals). Such an exercise, one could well hope, might extend one's powers of re-enactment, but it is a long step from that to increased self-knowledge (and a longer step still to political wisdom). The two things are different, and one does not necessarily entail the other; for, as mentioned in the Irish example, re-enactment of past fanaticism might lead not only to understanding what it was to be a fanatic, but also to fanaticism itself. Where Collingwood makes lofty claims about self-knowledge and political wisdom, he is at least operating in an interesting, conventionally plausible, and traditional area; but when he tries to pin down how it all works, the connections rattle.

'What history can bring to moral and political life is a trained eye for the situation in which one has to act'. (Perhaps, but why only history, and why history more than direct experience?) 'It was precisely because history offered us something altogether different from *rules*, namely *insight*, that it could afford us the help we need in diagnosing our moral and political problems'. Yes – there is something in it, but yes, the mix of optimism, conventional pieties and naive swank is embarrassing.

'All history is the history of thought', was Collingwood's profoundest slogan. Unlike the bad old history, the scissors-and-paste history based on shuffling snippets of evidence, he saw a good new history emerging which would engage the whole mind. 'There is nothing else except thought', he asserted rashly, 'that can be the subject of historical knowledge'; a point at which many jib. (What of the weather? What of disease?) Better perhaps to see what he means by thought. He seems to exclude unconscious thought and collective thought; large exceptions, these (though in his own *Roman Britain* his fault was relying too much on collective thought). At its simplest, 'historical knowledge is the re-enactment in the historian's mind of the thought whose history he is studying.' It is through re-enactment that we move from knowledge *that* something happened, to knowing *why*. Of course, this quest for virtual reality is re-enactment with a difference: of past thought but in a present context. The past thought lives in the present, but under the historian's control: the writer in his library both knows the past thought, and knows that it is past.

Here Collingwood elaborates his argument, to sort out this not very difficult issue. 'Nelson's thought, as Nelson thought it and as I re-think it, is certainly one and the same thought, and yet in some way there is not one and the same thought, there are two different thoughts ... What is the difference? The difference is one of context. To Nelson, it was a present thought; to me, it is a past thought – a "capsule" from the past "encapsulated" in the mind of the person thinking it in the present, but not part of their everyday existence.'

Well, what are the snags? Partly it is Collingwood's tone: insistent, inflated, self-important – the inevitable result of putting the historian not the past at the centre of what happens in historical study. Collingwood asserts an important finality, where he offers really only tentative exploration, with disorderly exceptions (like economic history) on every side. The snag of snags, however, concerns verification.

How does one know, or prove, that my re-enactment of the past is true, or truer (as opposed to more interesting or more intelligent) than yours? The answer is that it cannot be done. Re-enactment is necessary to the portrayal of meaning, rich and deep meanings especially, but where truth is concerned it hangs its head as little more than bright conjecture, intelligent intuition, suggestive hunch, and as such it can only be judged by the standards of brightness and suggestiveness.

Falsification, unlike verification, presents no difficulty. An imaginative re-enactment can readily be falsified. In Shakespeare's *Julius Caesar*, a clock strikes, thirteen centuries before clocks were invented. History-as-evidence, in its severity, tells what is not true; history-as-meaning, in its warm invitingness, usually leaves a multiplicity of possible truths, mine as good as yours. This is the black hole at the centre of historian-centred history. Those who look on history as a search for meaning, purvey not truths but the attitudes of one man to other men.

Collingwood should have spelled this out, separating falsification from verification, and verification from mere taste in explanation and re-enactment. But let us pay our respects. He was a philosopher who thought about history, and a practising historian who thought about philosophy. In this he has long stood almost alone. If his answers were not the Open Sesame that he thought, his questions will always raise fundamental issues. He was a sloganizer, a simplifier, an eluder of difficulties, a propagandist for history. But his slogans and simplifications have life, above all when compared with the unreflective professionalism of university historians in the first half of the twentieth century. In essentials, he is a contemporary mind for all involved in the social sciences. And like Marx, he matters even more when wrong than when right.

IV

History and Morality

'Thou shalt not judge,' said Christ: meaning that to do so was God's work alone. On the whole, there is little to add twenty centuries later, beyond raking over the embers of a dying controversy. These are shallow waters. There has always been a 'new' history.

On the one hand, in a way quite unrelated to any religious injunction, stands the argument that for cognitive reasons, we are not able to judge (or rather, judge justly); there is never enough to go on. One mind can never know another well enough to pronounce with any finality. And there is temptation, perhaps the hardest aspect of history to reconstruct – and are not the temptations of the powerful in particular of an intensity that the powerless can hardly conceive? And, even if all were known, the question would remain what, or whose, morality we should apply. That is one side of the argument.

The other side sounds, and is, just as sensible. Who needs to talk of the difficulties of ultimate judgment, it is said, when we seek not that but something altogether different – limited and interim judgments based on the portrayal of moral facts? Moral comment about past people, about their gluttony or laziness, is no different from comment on height or hair colour. Indeed, the omission of moral comment would in itself be a distortion (but moral comment like all other would be fallible, for laziness might be the product of a weakening infection like bilharzia).

Thus one must – not can, but must – make interesting moral comments about past people, evidence permitting, in the manner of a novelist. And one must report and explain what was said at the time by way of moral judgment – at the risk, no doubt, that such scrupulousness may give the heaviest weight to the least scrupulous and most condemnatory. This is the twist in the tail of the school of limited moral description and moral reporting. Not giving any judgment themselves, they will end up retailing the all too ultimate judgments of others.

For all, the question of what morality to apply remains perilous. The easy answer, that the Christian moral consensus is still largely with us, whether acknowledged or not, does not go far, such a consensus having always been thin on matters that concern historians. There are deep divergences in historical ethics, so deep that reconciliation seems inconceivable.

One criterion of morality is intention. A good man is one who has good intentions. A bad man is one who has bad motives or intentions. This fits well with private ethics. Indeed, it assumes that public ethics are an extension of the ethics of private life. Its drawbacks are that this is an improbable assumption, for public and private worlds differ so greatly, and because intentions, being inward things, are not so knowable as consequences.

The other criterion of morality is consequences. 'In politics it is consequences that matter': matter perhaps on the hugest scale, where it is no apology if disaster ensues, to say that one's intentions were of the best. There are historical situations where kindness is worse than murder, and goodwill the greatest atrocity. To grant independence to India was, among other things, the act of benevolent men, but to the 250,000 or more massacred as a result, consequences mattered more than intentions. Similarly, between the wars English political culture oozed goodwill; the consequence was that we nearly gave the world to Hitler. One can reverse the argument, and talk of bad intentions leading to good consequences; whatever the intentions behind the dropping of the atomic bomb, the consequence was a large saving of life, and perhaps of Japanese life, compared with the prospects had invasion taken place.

The morality of consequences often shocks. That is not the only objection to it, considered as a morality separate from that of private life (and of religion). It is that the idea of two opposed moralities running in tandem, but with uncertainty as to which applies on which occasion, is a recipe for muddle. Try, if you wish, to square the circle, by affirming that bad consequences are the result of bad, or negligent, or thoughtless intentions, and thus that all is ultimately intention after all, and you may think that your unified morality is discovered. But it is not so easy as that, for is intellectual error, the error of the man who holds that 2+2=5, the result of defective and culpable intention? The circle is not willing to be squared. History has to consider bad men who do good things, and good men who do bad things.

Perhaps there is a third school, transient and based on American fashion, which views historical morality in terms of how far social fairness is its governing principle: that is, morality as justice. Such a criterion has the singular merit of being compatible with both bad consequences, such as wrecking the economy, and with bad intentions, such as power mania. But, important though it is that the cries of 'human rights', 'fairness', and 'justice' should receive the same moral criticism as other slogans, this parenthesis concerns an oddity of current practice, not theory.

Even if it were possible to square all the philosophical circles, there would remain perhaps an even greater impasse, that of historical relativism. There are limp attempts to say that morality is something universal, that murder (in particular) is not excused in any time or place. Perhaps, but murder apart? No institution has found wider acceptance over a longer period than slavery, unless it be torture. No great religion, no great teacher, opposed either. Christianity did not abhor slavery; even slaves did not wish for slavery to end. Civilized men, in free elections, voted overwhelmingly to become slaves, when given the chance early last century. Slavery is the norm, from which we have only recently deviated; how then do the deviants judge the morality of the norm? To talk of judging the past in its own terms may sound the height of fair play, but if it means applying a morality that we hold profoundly wrong, what purpose is served beyond practice in insincerity?

Where moral judgment is linked to a broad political conviction of today, such as feminism, collectivism, anti-imperialism or anti-racism, the difficulty is that such views are so extremely modern. Adopting standards based on them, means a blanket moral condemnation of almost everything before 1900 (at very earliest), except perhaps in cases where one can discern the faint beginnings of the present day. The gulf between a liberal, democratic, secular, collectivist, feminist present, and a non-liberal, non-democratic, non-secular, non-collectivist, non-feminist past grows more impassable by the year. The idea of a common historical morality is a will-o'-the-wisp, because our time has deviated so far from the human norm. And to say, chin high, that the human norm was wrong, and that we are the first moral generation, though it would have the merit of honestly expressing the student mind, otherwise serves no productive purpose.

Even within our own century, we have wild variations in moral assessments. Consider the Union of South Africa. Its creation in 1910, which effectively ensured its control by the Boers, was long seen by the enlightened as a triumph of liberal statesmanship on the part of England, an example, perhaps the very best example, of reconciliation between conqueror and conquered.

The black peoples of South Africa were, for most educated men, and for most liberal-minded men, invisible men. Only much later did doubts creep in about the wisdom of handing South Africa over to one group, and that an inflexible one; but when the doubts came, they soon hardened into the equally inflexible moral mould called anti-apartheid.

Those passing moral judgment on South Africa this century have believed that they were inspired by an enduring principle of inclusiveness. In each case, inclusiveness turned out to be a new way of leaving people out. The passage of time, even of quite short periods of time, deals cruelly with the most profoundly certain moral consensus, the most incontestable principle, the most apparently timeless of political and social values.

Values do not have to be avoided, for they do not even exist. Nobody knows what they are. Nobody can specify their content. Nobody has the authority to declare their nature. No text, no teacher, lays them down. There is no list of such things anywhere. They are not in the encyclopedia. They are a generality made up of no particulars. They are not prohibitions, as in the Ten Commandments. They are not commands. They do not connect with serious criteria of intention and consequence.

Values may be part of the factual past, part of its sociology; if so, being factual, they can provide no overarching criterion of assessment. Facts alone can never pronounce or pass judgment on facts. The function of 'values' in moral assessment (the inverted comma is deserved, for the usage is novel) is to encourage vague pretensions with no intellectual basis. Moral judgments in history cannot be founded on 'values', as if these were anything more than the opinions of the moment, unless we know what 'values' are: and nobody does.

V

'Kings and Battles': Holocaust Blindness and the Heritage School

No educational commonplace is more acceptable, or more traditional, than that history 'should not just be about kings and battles'. None more constantly parades itself as a novel truth struggling against a blinkered view of the world. Yet its roots are venerable.

The famous third chapter of Macaulay's *History of England* (1848-60) is one starting point. The novels of Sir Walter Scott, especially those depicting the social history of Scotland, are certainly another. The names of Thomas Carlyle (1795-1881) and Michelet deserve honourable mention. Burckhardt's *The Civilization of the Renaissance in Italy: An Essay* (1860) was a masterpiece of imaginary social history. The 'new history' was already old when in Victorian times John Richard Green (1837-83) wrote the immensely popular *Short History of the English People* (1874) depicting the common things of common men.

Nearer our own time G.M. Trevelyan, having first made his name as a political historian, wrote the bestselling *English Social History: A Survey of Six Centuries* (1944). This reached a mass audience such as no political history of England has ever reached. To play down battles, in the midst of the greatest battle the world had yet seen, was no mean feat, yet Trevelyan did it to acclaim.

In our own day, the leading exponent, as theorist, controversialist, and practitioner, is Raphael Samuel, who summed up the case against 'kings and battles' in the educational debates of the Eighties and Nineties, and it is his arguments that require reply.

It would be pleasant if history were or could be about man's peaceful heritage, his ways of earning a living, life at local level and on the small scale. For Green to take this view in 1874, in the long Victorian peacetime, in an island hardly invaded since 1066, was plausible indeed. Events since 1874, and the diminution first of England, then of Europe, in the scale of things, unfortunately have not lent support to the National Trust view of history. The twentieth century has turned out so much worse than expected (and not just up to the deaths of Hitler or of Stalin, if one considers humanity as a whole), and in essentially political ways at that, that some revision of the ways in which we can see the past needs to be considered. As the twentieth century ends, there are simply too many dead bodies on the stage for one to be quite easy with the softer historical approaches: history as nostalgia for what was good, history as lament over what was bad (the National Trust version inverted), history as a search for the quaintly specific in everyday life and work (the oral history tradition), history as sensitivity to growth in everyday welfare (the collectivist or social democratic tradition). Tenderness towards social classics such as John Galt's *Annals of the Parish*, Robert Roberts's *The Classic Slum*, and Flora Thompson's *Lark Rise to Candleford* should still leave us in questioning mood about the relationship between such apparently stable microcosms and the wider world of national and international force and power.

In parenthesis, let us note one component of social history as normally taught which presents few difficulties. This involves the study of government social policy, an aspect long prominent in the growth of the subject.

Logically, this is really no different from other departmental outgrowths of archival political history. Historically, it tends to overrate the importance of social policy on the governmental menu of the past. Politically, it may tend to collectivist self-congratulation. But its position is in practice uncontentious; so let logic sleep, and let the history of social policy be. Not much more than terminology links it with the history of past everyday life (*Alltagsgeschichte*) and with the history of past social structures – and the link between the two latter, between essentially German and essentially French approaches, may not always be too clear.

It would be rash to suppose that social history in its various traditions has any essential underlying unity. Like everything else, social history has to be seen in the light of what has happened historically. Had there been but one World War this century, one might just concede that the study of 'kings and battles' was almost a cultural escape from more concealed forms of social violence like bad housing, tuberculosis, crop failure, and the rest. Two World Wars, however, tip the balance; 'kings and battles' have evidently not withered as the Victorians hoped. History is horrible and its horror is more political than social: especially this century. It is not intellectual argument, but experience on the grand scale which for the present controls our sense of the place of force in history.

What does 'kings and battles', used as a slogan, mean when decoded? It is an eyecatching but necessary shorthand for the role of power in society. Of course, for most of the past, 'kings and battles' meant kings and battles. In modern times, however, 'kings', to take the most obvious case, means presidents or prime ministers. Battles may remain battles, whether fought, or (more likely) unfought, as in the case of the Cold War; but brute force has innumerable dimensions.

It may, today, mean conflict in globalized financial markets. It may mean the conquest of national societies by an international business aristocracy. It may mean the predatory exercise of power by local elites which sometimes passed for decolonization. It may mean the cultural conquest inherent in television becoming a globalized rather than indigenous medium. It may mean that modern post-manual society, by the very nature of its own progress, cannot avoid creating a class excluded from its modernity, with whom it is in barely concealed and deepening war. Force remains at the centre of history. Wherever the strong defeat the weak, 'kings and battles' are very much to the point.

How much to the point, is a matter of subjective assumptions and attitudes; a historically true answer is intrinsically impossible (though had the twentieth century been more like the nineteenth, the range of plausible answers would be different). But it is not plausible today, as it perhaps was when Green wrote, to see conflict as unusual. In a famous passage, the sociologist Dahrendorf remarks that there is no objective way of choosing whether conflict (or force) or consensus is primary. Commenting on exactly the same evidence, writers who adhere to one of these two outlooks will produce directly contradictory interpretations. One sees the world – whether the social world, or the economic world, or the society of states, is unimportant – as a happy family which sometimes quarrels.

The other school sees a quarrelling family which is sometimes happy. The argument is not about evidence. To some, the glass is half full; to others, it is half empty. To the first school, consensus equals normality, and it is conflict which needs explaining; to the latter school, consensus is the historical exception. A minor point is that it is all too easy for English historians in particular to take consensus for granted, or to focus on the arcane form of ritualized consensus called party conflict. Being English is no help; England's 'special route' through its past has left a sense of immunity to catastrophe.

Catastrophe and normality, catastrophe and everyday life, 'kings and battles' and everyday life, have merged into each other in most countries since 1914; if not in accomplished fact, then in expectation and probability. In the 1990s, they do not appear quite such opposite and separable categories as in the 1890s. Everyday life includes 'kings and battles'; 'kings and battles' in part determine everyday life (consider Yugoslavia). In some minor but intensely concentrated cases, the permeation of everyday life by antagonisms affecting the whole society is obvious: antagonisms constitute and define the society. Ask a Pole, a Serb, an Alsatian, a Basque, an Ulsterman, a Palestinian, a South African, above all a Jew, about their modern history; the inevitability of collectivist liberal democracy, and the apparently autonomous patterns of everyday life within it, will not be their first thought. Here the temptation for us in any millennial stocktaking is to relegate 'kings and battles' to the category of tragic exception; to say that it is a matter of locality, and untypical localities at that; and to consider, as we so firmly did in the 1920s, that civilization has left enormities behind. (The average European frontier is much more recent than the average African frontier; which is typical?) A millennial stocktaking based on recent hopefulness is as likely to be wrong as one made at any earlier date; and it will almost certainly show signs of holocaust blindness.

Holocaust blindness makes heritage history possible. One form of blindness is indifference to the catastrophes that England should, as it were, have undergone, a lack of feeling for its sheer good luck and abnormality, not just in escaping from the European mainstream, but also in departing from its own inherent probabilities. Another form of blindness is indifference to holocausts, or to world wars, a tacit acceptance that they are mere irregularities or blips which do not much disturb the longer rhythms of history.

Consider what might have been the normal path of English development. It is something that should ever float before us. The pattern could without strangeness have been this. The Black Death would have shortly been followed by the Spanish conquest of the sixteenth century, a relatively bloodless imposition of rationality, but involving a novel consistency in taxation which led to sporadic revolts such as the Iconoclasm of Norwich. More seriously, it left England without the option of playing the part of a demilitarized satellite. In the Thirty Years War, no less than four foreign armies contended for mastery of English soil, and the putting of Bristol to the sword entered folk memory.

The Great Peace under the Wallensteins restored stability, until the collapse of state credit after defeat in the French war, and the concession to France of its 'natural frontier' on the Thames. The subsequent abdication led to intermittent civil war between the gentry republic of Citizen Burke, and the Navy Radicals, ending only in the protectorate of Marshal Wellesley and entry into the French mercantilist system. Despite disinterested government, England under the Wellesleys, deprived of its trade, moved inexorably towards demographic disaster, exacerbated by reliance on a single crop as it became the granary of a rapidly industrializing France.

The wheat rust and mass starvation of the Wet Years initiated catastrophic depopulation. Politically, failure of French relief efforts inspired obsessive nationalism centred on liberating the so-called 'lost' French province south of the Thames, a movement abruptly ended by the flight of the Whig earls to Madeira and the internment of Gladstone on St Helena.

Next century, the determining event was the German war.

Long-standing English scientific backwardness made it structurally inevitable that Germany would be first with the atomic bomb. The clinical elimination of Leeds and Sheffield brought speedy surrender, and at least saved England from invasion. Indeed, no event did more to bring England into the European Union, even if at the time it seemed another sad chapter in England's troubled history.

The concoction above may raise eyebrows. Nevertheless, it follows from structure and probability more closely than what actually happened. It is far less arbitrary than such improbabilities as 1066, 1588, and 1688. Successful invasion was always more probable than not (and France today retains highly unnatural 'natural frontiers' in once German lands). No natural law of botany makes corn immune and the potato not. In general, although the above concoction is brewed from recognizable elements in European history, it takes a milder form. If catastrophic, it is so in a way that many nations would give much for.

English audiences are liable not only to underestimate the place of catastrophe abroad, but also to avert their gaze from the disastrous nature of a re-imagined English history based on probability. What actually happened, is in this case a distraction and a temptation: it opens the door to a safely autonomous heritage history of, as Raphael Samuel puts it, pioneering studies of horses, of sporting prints and landscape art, of the opening page of *Black Beauty*, of the folk and folk life. (Samuel, to be fair, does recognize the arcadian, or sanitized, roots of much 'history from below' without giving much hope that it can easily be dispelled.) Much of social history is safe history, in which the terrible does not happen (the two world wars, for instance, are domesticated by metamorphosing them into periods of accelerated social change, mostly benign), and safe history is itself unsafe.

Because history on a small scale obscures the large event, which holocausts necessarily are, 'history from below' may tend to reinforce a certain holocaust blindness in the English mind which is already there anyway for quite different reasons, some entirely honourable. One, obviously, is the legitimate wish to assert that the Jewish holocaust was the only one worthy of the name. If only it did so stand alone; if only one did not sense a European-centred-

ness here; if only public information on the general run of holocausts were reasonably balanced, which it is not; if only the
singularity, or uniqueness, of the Jewish holocaust (whether numerically, or in horror) made all else bearable to contemplate; if
only one could look at this matter, as one cannot, with reasonably
balanced amounts of information, and without the political necessity to rebut those who deny simple matters of record. But there is
a price to be paid for the Anglo-Saxon or western wish to assert the
primacy of the Jewish holocaust. Should such an assertion imply
that this event was so extraordinary, so unparalleled, that that
was it for all time, it delivers us in complete unwariness to those
forces that its upholders most wish to condemn.

Dwelling on the Jewish holocaust exaggerates the goodness of
mankind. The English mind perhaps does not consider sufficiently
the multiplicity and normality of awfulness, the uncertainty of the
borderline between extermination and warfare, the Polish and
Yugoslav understanding of their own national destruction, and
extra-European ethnic cleansing, as in the Sudan and Indonesia.
Indeed, the first European discovery, of the Canary islands, resulted in the first ethnic cleansing, of the natives of the islands, not
one surviving; the first large-scale settlement, of Mexico, resulted
in the depopulation of the New World, through epidemics but in no
less 'political' a context, by tens of millions. In the story of European expansion, ecological holocausts have been pretty normal.

It is memorably vague on the Soviet Union's double experience
of massacre, from Stalin and from Hitler. (Politically induced
famine is less memorable than gas chambers; intention, scale, and
effect were similar.) It is uninformed about those aspects of the
Spanish Civil War where party and class cleansing resembled
aspects of the holocaust, and all the more so because of the distort-
ing educational emphasis placed on Orwell's account of a petty
factional sideshow in the Barcelona streets. Knowledge of the
non-Jewish holocaust of prisoners-of-war and deportees in wartime Germany is shadowy, while without some understanding of
the German non-combatant holocaust of 1944-5 there will be no
true reconciliation. 'Kings and battles' determined why a quarter
of West German families live where they do: a long walk from their
ancestral homes. Where China stands in the extermination league

tables at any point is not a matter of wide present curiosity, Tibet apart, but were it to become so, the numbers involved would necessarily be large indeed by any western standard.

Mass deaths are in this century fairly normal; perhaps they always were. Mass deaths are essentially political and have to be explained in political terms – in terms of 'kings and battles'. The historian Eric Hobsbawm, an optimist, gives an estimate of 183 million for those dying from political causes in this century so far. This does not leave much space for the non-political 'everyday life'.

The objection to the heritage school of history is not just that it diminishes violence, war, and suffering as phenomena of a whole society, and not particularly rare ones. It is, more widely, that 'history from below' does not unite the different strands in the story, but unweaves what should be inseparable. That 'history from below' is so at ease with personal economic hardship, but not with collective death, only compounds its individualism, selectivity and prescriptiveness. How often it becomes a lament over Oppression down the Ages, how rarely it extols the benefits of an ordered inequality, and how trivially it wrings its hands over finding the (truistic) presence of 'social control', a distemper which like stress was invented within living memory.

'History from below' is wrong in much the same way as 'high politics' on its own is wrong or insufficient. When upholders of 'history from below' say 'high politics' or 'kings and battles' are insufficient, it is really themselves they condemn, for in both cases the part is no substitute for the whole, and the whole must be the sum of all the forces at work within a society, and probably outside too. Thus, the social biography of the poor no more makes sense, than one of the rich as a class; each exists only in relation to the other.

The same for 'high politics', a term sometimes involving historical faction fighting. First, the case for. High politics happens; politicians and states do relate in complex and opaque, but ultimately explicable, patterns. Such activity takes place in a political world whose ritualized meanings are elusive even to the wider ruling class from which practitioners of high politics come. There is an inner code to be cracked, mystifications to be demystified; and since privilege and mystification are closely entangled, no friend of the People can object to demystification. Politics needs explaining historically, in terms of what politicians do.

Present politics cannot be understood; past politics can. The evidence, in terms of access to sources, improves with time. We knew hardly anything of Brezhnev; a little of Stalin; much more of Lenin; and of Marx, almost everything. In the western world, past politics is probably best documented in the nineteenth century – better, perhaps, than ever it will be again. Politics, as an academic subject, is history without the evidence, or, discourteously, yester-day's newspapers plus some useful but limited spheres such as opinion polls and psephology.

Now the case against. The 'high politics' approach gives a false picture of high politics itself. Politicians operated within a struc-tured society – structured by its institutional and economic structure (which we find easy to remember) and by its values (easily forgotten). And, whatever these actually were (which of course matters), those within high politics, especially from some time in the nineteenth century, have had their own theoretical perceptions, possibly wildly wrong, of how society as a whole might be moulded and what course it was taking and ought to take.

There is a subjective sociology within the minds of leading men, which may bear a very limited relation to any objective sociology of how groups and classes actually relate. In any case, 'high politics' cannot be understood by isolating elite activity from the total sociology of the society within which it takes place. In practice, one of the achievements of the 'high politics' approach has been to relate the highly coded activities and personal relationships among leading men to the structure and beliefs of society generally, and in particular to class, real and perceived.

Still, classes, structures, value systems, the whole sociological apparatus, do not do certain things. They do not take decisions. They do not write letters. They do not speak or plot or manoeuvre or reunite Germany. They do not inspire. The world of political decisions is a very silent, individual world, to be explained one person, one mind, one letter at a time. They may say that diplo-matic history is but the record of what one clerk wrote to another clerk; the number of lives turning on his correspondence, unknown though both it and he may indeed be, makes it a phenomenon of true importance.

VI

Causes in History

Causes do not exist.

Or rather, they exist only in a form so general, or, contrarily, so particular and subjective, as to require little attention.

The cause of an event, say some, is all that leads up to an event: all. There is nothing antecedent to an event that is not in some measure, however minute, its cause, in the sense that without it, something different would have happened.

On this view, to say that something is a cause, is no real help (even if true) because so, in varying degrees, is everything else. Causality becomes an infinitely diffuse process. It is narrative taken to ideal lengths.

The cause of an event, say others, is a matter of almost arbitrary choice. We select, from the infinity of possible causes, those that we, shall we say, fancy.

Here the subjectivity is blatant. What we choose to name as a cause, or (but let us hope not) *the* cause, is no more a cause than all the other circumstances that we choose not to name. And, if subjectivity is blatant, distortion is certain, or nearly so, taking a run of cases. 'Cause' is a way of overplaying the novel, at the expense of the static or continuing; the piquant, at the expense of the difficult; the enlivening, at the expense of the dull; the definite, at the expense of the indefinable. Causes become eye-catching labels. Used in this way, 'cause', far from being a matter of scientific investigation, belongs to the department of literary art and indeed rhetoric.

The extreme case of this is where a great event is made to depend upon one that is both random and minute. This is the historical equivalent of the meteorological theory that 'the flapping of a butterfly's wings in the Amazon produces a thunderstorm in London'. Had Cleopatra's nose been a centimetre different in length, would the future of the Roman Empire have been different? Did a chance sea fog, by allowing the enemy to blockade southern Russia, cause the Russian Revolution? Such questions raise no issue of truth, for their sole purpose is so obviously to make the reader sit up. The vocabulary may sound philosophical, but the sole purpose is literary effect.

Cause is simply the wrong word to use. It raises hopes of an unattainable accuracy. Its connotations are of the impact of one billiard ball upon another, an idea that may be seen at its worst in that insidious phrase, cause and effect. Life could not be less like that. Unique (but also complex) historical situations and events do not have knowable, predictable, and replicable causes and consequences, in a way that causes regularly beget consequences in science. Stick to the idea that historical events are unique (and thus cannot have causes in the easy and simple sense of observable, replicable regularities) and all hopes of specifying something as elusive as a particular unique cause wither.

Translating the word 'cause' into the supposed everyday language of common sense is of little help. To say that to cause something is to bring it about, to make it happen, or be responsible for it happening, does little to explain what 'cause' might mean in a search for the causes of infinitely complex situations (the Industrial Revolution, the origins of the First World War, the English Civil War) where discussion is most abundant. The language of the common sense equivalents of 'cause' is as woolly and porous as that of 'cause' itself.

Common enmities make strange bedfellows. The idea that cause is the objective total of antecedent events, and the view that it is a matter of subjective choice (perhaps a necessity of literary art, perhaps at very most a necessity of human understanding, though not a necessity inherent in nature) are outwardly at opposite ends of the spectrum. Yet it is not so much what they affirm, as what they jointly deny, that matters. Neither leaves any room for the idea of particular objective causes, as when one billiard ball strikes another. This, the middle ground of causality, they combine to reject: causality in its everyday usage, causality as the examiner understands it. This attack from both sides on examiners' causality is slaughter indeed.

And yet there is a tail to the argument. There are, as usual, two sides to the case, if not two equal sides. Whichever of the extreme theories of causality we adopt, the tremendously general or the thumpingly specific, we add nothing to knowledge. We intermingle a causality which explains everything, with a causality which explains nothing – all the while using a vocabulary of cause and effect which at least suggests that in the billiard ball sense, A can cause B. This state of affairs will not do.

For a start, it is wholly impractical in one of its components. Well it is for the philosophers, for the notion is theirs, to speak of cause as a total description of antecedent circumstances. In theory, they are right. In practice, historians know that such a totality cannot be assembled; so selection and abstraction there must be, even if it goes against the philosophical grain, because of the natural limits upon human understanding.

There is another justification for the philosophically illusory search for particular objective causes. What appears to be a search for causes, is really an argument about the relative proportions or weight to be given to different elements in a situation. Long may such debate continue; but if only because one is constructing a landscape, the discussion should not masquerade as an inquiry into causality.

The great philosopher Professor Karl Popper helpfully describes causality as 'a typical metaphysical hypostatization of a well-justified methodological rule'. Quite; and historians have to balance the first half of his comment (causality has no real existence) with his second (it helps to behave as though it did exist).

The remotest, least obvious shore of causality is perhaps its most productive source of insight. It concerns the counter-factual, the study of what did not happen, immortalized by Sherlock Holmes in his phrase about the curious case of the dog that did not bark in the night-time.

The issue raised is whether B could have happened, had A been absent. Or, with a slight difference of inflection, had A (say, American slavery) persisted, could B still have happened? Nobody can know, for A was not in fact absent, or left to persist. We are in the realm of insight, however quantitatively presented, not truth or knowledge. Still, if we persuade ourselves that without A, B would have been impossible, we have come to see A as one of a bundle of causes; a position leaning to the idea of objective particular causes of the billiard ball kind, but best judged by whether its novelty sharpens insight.

Explanation is a better term than cause. It has less linear overtones, which is all to the good. Explanation leads away from determinism, while maintaining intelligibility. Explanation keeps the door open to a necessary and desirable woolliness, yet leaves interesting and real choices open. The stultifying search for the causes of the Industrial Revolution, becomes an explanation of the proportions of elements of early industrialism. What is in a word? Much.

In particular, where 'cause' tends to look backward in time, explanation divides into two branches, genetic (or explanation with reference to the past) and functional (or explanation with reference to the present), leaving free choice of emphasis in any particular case.

In genetic explanation, one traces developments backward in time. The history of mathematics is a prime example. What mathematicians do is mainly explicable in relation to what past mathematicians have done. There is no necessity about this. Had Louis XIV ennobled mathematicians or Mao exterminated them, the history of mathematics could be told mainly as a story of the relation between mathematicians and their own time. But, as it befell, it makes better sense to explain mathematical activity in terms of its own past.

In functional explanation, one looks foremost at the relations between those in their own time. Naval history is a case in point. Encrusted though it may be with a rich past, to explain the behaviour of fleets in war one looks mainly to the present, to what the enemy is or does.

In the case of political history especially, the distinction between genetic and functional explanation is sometimes helpful. It clarifies approaches to a question, though without laying down any methodological imperative. It broadens the range of explanations that can be offered; the present (as it then was) can be explained either in terms of its present, or its past. The contemporary situation in which politicians, or parties or states, find themselves, the interplay of antagonisms which creates stability, is usually not best explained by reference to previous events. Where politics, domestic or international, is outwardly confrontational, there is often a kind of hidden connivance whereby the actions of one party are the obverse of its opponent. Here explanation must be in terms of the total contemporary situation; party biography, for instance, like biography, and like the study of the foreign policy of one power on its own, risks not being attuned to the strong element of reciprocity in political situations.

Such remarks are tentative, and prompted by the mechanical dullness and querulous vanity which the search for causes produces in historical education. 'Cause' is a constriction on historical thought; let it be unbound.

VII

Bias in History

History is about evidence, and evidence flagrantly distorts. There is a bias in the creation of evidence, and a bias in the survival of evidence. There may be a bias in access to what survives, too. There is a bias towards the important (and self-important), a political bias to winners against losers, a bias towards the stable and against the unstable, and perhaps a deliberate censorship of the past by the past on top of that. Before we even get to modern historians, distortion is built into the very nature of history.

This suggests a simple rule. No evidence, no history; imperfect evidence, imperfect history. Against such stark considerations, purity of motive on the part of historians today faces an uphill task. The distortions in evidence that are already there, cannot be brushed away with a broom called objectivity.

But – our culture has a bias against bias. In a truth-centred culture, bias means departure from the scientific model. Indeed, it is seen as meaning departure from morality itself. To accuse someone of bias is to hit hard. And, worse, the word has an ugly ring to it; let no one believe that lack of euphony makes no odds. (Call bias commitment, and it might be a different story.) That bias might be a means to truth, is not easy to say in our supposedly truth-centred world.

Nine out of ten students, then, would be against bias; would indeed be rather horrified by the thought. That must be our starting-point. And at once mountainous difficulties confront us. The first great difficulty is purely practical. It is the extreme difficulty of naming any historical writers who are not well and truly biased. Worse still, their bias is not some shameful blot upon their reputations, but no small part of their reputation itself.

A Gibbon who lacked a sadistic bias against Christianity would be insipid; a Macaulay who was fair to Tories, unthinkable.

The second great difficulty, if we wish to rule that bias is bad, comes from the sociology of knowledge. It is perhaps something of an oddity that in discussions of bias, we always begin (and usually end) by looking at this or that individual writer and his individual quirks, while paying little or no attention to the general forces shaping the body of writers as a whole. And indeed there are reasons for this avoidance of overmuch sociological determinism. For one thing, at certain times in the past (though not many), historical writing may have been a heterogeneous, miscellaneous, fractured thing, not lending itself to general explanation. That is not the case today, when history is a professional activity almost monopolized by academics. For another, the sociology of knowledge always irritates. How, they cry, can my most intimate, my most personal moments of mental life result from some broad sociological forces of which I am hardly aware? Outrage ensues, and always will.

Historians today – and probably the great majority of historians who have ever lived, live today – exist in a definite sociological situation. Writers of history are, in Europe and elsewhere, state employees; in America, a workforce, albeit within large organizations like those fostered by public collectivism. They are not rentiers, landowning gentry, monkish scribes, churchmen, practitioners of public affairs, or intellectual hunter-gatherers. If they were, we should comment on it, and so we should on their being public employees.

The question, at its simplest, is not what difference it makes but whether it is so; and it is so, despite the presence in varying degrees of many trappings and vestiges of independence, the afterglow of gentlemanliness, and even the sensibility of the 'free intellectual', diminish though these do by the year. Yes, the production of historical truth has become ultimately a sub-department of the collectivist state; it has one, single, definite sociological location – and for that not to imply bias of some sort would need quite majestic powers of disconnection from surrounding circumstance.

Historians today are not holders of power – power over men, over money, over opinion. They live among the foothills of society, where they engage anxiously in downward social mobility. They see very little of power in their own lives; they do not catch its reflections in the lives of others. From the life of action in its modern form – business – they are quite especially remote. Their disconnection from things, their want of rootedness, their poverty of commitment, are those of the minor official class the world over. History may have changed; but historians, as a class, have changed more.

Present historians experience less than past historians. This narrowing of life they call professionalism, as indeed in a technical sense it is. Professionalism is the positive name given to a negative fact (and social novelty): the single historical career from youth to age, lived within large academic institutions, based on a single academic subject, worthy indeed and commendable but ill matched with the task of understanding other existences.

But what has all this to do with bias? Well, living on a state salary, while looking forward to an index-linked pension, rather than by selling books, is unlikely to weaken one's collectivist outlook. The payroll historian is likely to look with tender sympathy upon the general system which produces salaries for people like him to live on, just as in the days of gentry scholarship, few raised their voices to condemn rental income from land. In broad terms, historians rightly see their well-being as connected with the big state, the high tax economy, and the acceptance of definitions of progress linked to these. Historians of recent centuries visibly approve the growth of the hand which has fed them. They may be right to do so; indeed probably are. But when they mix description and prescription, make 'social reform' the measure of all things, and deride market forces, it is appropriate to recall that, left to the market, there would be few historians and little history. Whether it is bias, or just a subtle convergence of view between paymaster and paid, it works rather like bias.

There is another aspect to state-paid history. The outlook of the minor official leans to grumpiness, to the cultivation of an opposition mentality, to failure to sympathize with those in responsibility – for in a collectivist world all mistakes come from above. What supply and demand are in the world of market forces, so mandatory clamour and dissatisfaction are within a collectivist polity, each part of which must intone fervent anthems of 'More!' The academic mind sees itself as ill-paid and under-rewarded, in the sense of not having enough for habits of life which it affects to scorn; and from this, some sense of critical sourness will long arise, some unwillingness to accept the normality of failure in others. Whether we call it bias or not, the relaxing experience of easy and natural success – that root of forgiveness – will have corrupted few historians' hearts.

Payroll history is here, has been here for some time, and will not go away. It bears no resemblance to the flourishing literary history of before 1900. It must have some inner bias of its own, even if it is still hard to define. It is a new phenomenon in the sociology of knowledge – an economic lobby charged with the production of truth, a profession supposed to look from the outside on great social changes of which its own existence forms a minute part. (As well might one ask teeth to give a neutral view of dentistry.) Of course there are colourful freebooters and subtle quietists who follow no rule. That does not mean that general tendencies cannot be observed.

As Mr Gladstone rightly said, in the old days one bribed individuals, but in modern democracy one bribes whole classes. Or, as Koestler put it, a Communist who is a deputy will have more in common with a non-Communist deputy, than he will have with a Communist who is not a deputy. Sociologically, the professional historian of today, with his pension, is deeply 'inside', deeply encased in something, some form of stability and predictability and also limitation, in a way that will both define his habits of thought and separate him from his predecessors. Something rather big has happened, and squeaks of pained non-recognition cannot regain for him a position of entire freedom in the sociology of knowledge, the position of freebooter or lone adventurer. So it is with bias. In the old days, bias was primarily individual, a product of personal commitment. As such, it might be a path to understanding. Under modern conditions, bias is more likely to be socially determined, and the face it wears will be that of the minor official.

VIII

The Whig Interpretation of History:
Why Butterfield Matters

The nineteenth-century revolution in academic or university history, for all that it wore its objectivity on its sleeve, was like all history inspired by and intent on promoting a set of beliefs. In other words, though technically immeasurably superior and more scientific than the preceding school of literary history, it none the less resembled it in being ideological.

In English terms, it believed that English history was the story of progress, that parliament spelled progress, that parliament, even if not central, ought to have been, and that eighteenth-century parliaments and parties were recognizable forerunners of English politics about 1910. Where Tories and monarchs embarrassed the stage, it was only to be hissed off as villains of the piece. There were sub-plots, but in the same tone: the victory of the courts of law over the king's arbitrary power (seen as an excuse, not for palliating, but for wholly ignoring the horryifying injustice of the legal system), the Reformation as a step – a key word, suffused with ideology – towards modern freedoms, and the odious and corrupt nature of pre-Gladstonian patronage.

There was a 'Whig philosophy' of history. Its hallmark was explaining the present in terms of the past, and implying that the present was better than the past. But all shades of opinion shared this outlook to some degree, the Tory Anglican Bishop Stubbs (1825-1901) who more than any other man created English medieval history as an academic subject, no less than the Liberal Dissenter S.R. Gardiner (1829-1902), a descendant of Cromwell, and the creator of the narrative history of 1603-1660. Stubbs's *The Constitutional History of England in its Origin and Development* (1874-8), though partly a churchman's reflection on the place of sin in history, was, as its very title makes clear, organized around the characteristic Whig idea that 'great oaks from little acorns grow'.

The academic revolution produced beliefs. It produced much professional history of the highest quality. But, after its Victorian founding fathers, it simply became rather dull. It tended not to produce historians who embodied what was alert in the national culture (itself not a formidable quantity). When the neo-liberal movement loosely called Bloomsbury wanted history, it had to turn to non-historians to write it: the economist Keynes on contemporary history, the philosopher Bertrand Russell on the history of thought, the literary critic Lytton Strachey on the Victorians. There was no intellectual excitement, or even colour, in university history, fiercely dull, proudly inward-looking, attuned to a secular professionalism; the period 1900-1950 lacks great names (and even after 1950, so much attention focused on the history of sub-cultures, that the lack of any new total picture muted or fragmented ideological challenge).

The great historians of the twentieth century in England were two: Namier and Butterfield. Both stood out the more, because of the surrounding dullness. Both were of world-wide reputation and influence. Both affected the general cultural climate far outside their own field of history, in the way that Keynes, T.S. Eliot, and Wittgenstein did. Both focused on the eighteenth century, the nineteenth century remaining largely *terra incognita* until the 1960s. Both destroyed, rather than constructed. What they destroyed was the stately historical edifice of the Victorian and post-Victorian world-picture, the apparently immutable canonical version of the stages of European history enshrined by Lord Acton in the 1890s in the *Cambridge Modern History*. It is not because of having produced historical masterpieces that Namier and Butterfield matter, but because, more unusually, they altered the way men thought about history so that nothing was ever quite the same again.

Both were outsiders, culturally and as individuals. Both were destructive critics of English pieties. Both left little standing of what had gone before. Both used their allegedly past-centred philosophy of history to spike enemy guns in the present.

Were they right? In factual terms, broadly yes. If a historical philosophy of progress should emerge again, it will not be based on parliamentarianism or protestantism, or the idea that Reformation and Renaissance were rationalism new-born from its shell. Such querying of Lord Acton's drama of the unfolding of medieval into modern constituted useful correction, on the largest scale, but not the fundamental change in method that Butterfield called for, even if he found it impossible to embody.

Sir Herbert Butterfield (1900-79), Master of Peterhouse, Professor of History at Cambridge 1944-68, Vice-Chancellor of Cambridge, was not the typical Establishment figure he sounds.

Butterfield was a very unusual kind of Christian, where Namier was a politicized Jew. He was a Christian outsider: his mother belonged to the Plymouth Brethren, his father was Methodist, and he himself preached in local Methodist chapels from 17 to 36.

In *The Whig Interpretation of History*, published in 1931, Butterfield argued not just that the past should be studied for its own sake, but that it had usually not been so studied; that history should be a total history of life, not only of political life; that abridgement of the complexity of the past was one great means of distortion; that hindsight was the other.

Some of his views became maxims, indeed slogans. 'It takes a year to do a year'. 'It takes a hundred years to recapture what was common knowledge at the time'. 'The men of 1807 could not foresee 1808' (though they may well have attached importance to thinking that they foresaw it, which would itself be a fact of some weight). The discovery of a single new fact, he asserted, might mean the reinterpretation of a whole episode, starting from the beginning.

Whig history, he argued, 'studies the past with reference to the present'. It was not merely the result of partisanship, but 'an unexamined habit of mind that any historian may fall into'. Still, crude partisanship had played its part: 'it is astonishing to what an extent the historian has been protestant, progressive, and Whig'. It tended 'to praise revolutions provided that they have been successful', and 'to produce a story which is the ratification if not the glorification of the present'. Our own age, he reminded us, 'is not the Absolute to which the men of the Reformation are only relative'; rather, 'all ages are equidistant from God'. The present, indeed, even if we knew more about it, is narrow, fleeting, an inconsiderable dot in the future's past. Suppose, however, that one wished to explain the present, the only guiding principle would be that 'it is nothing less than the whole of the past which has produced the whole of the present', and not just by means of a 'cosmic scheme of good and evil in conflict'.

Butterfield protested against the ideology, the false judgments, and the unseen and unrecognized distortions implicit in the conventional periodization of history. He opposed 'a popular view that is still not quite eradicated – the view that the Middle Ages represented a period of darkness when man was kept tongue-tied by authority – a period against which the Renaissance was the reaction and the Reformation the great rebellion'. It was here, not in the handling of minute detail, that professional historians fell down: 'it is over large periods and in reference to the great events in European history that the Whig view holds hardest and holds longest'.

Butterfield was not calling for 'Tory' history to replace Whig: a history written through the eyes of those who stood for stability. Nor did he want a mechanical synthesis: 'we do not gain true history by merely adding the speech for the prosecution to the speech for the defence'. Again, he did not want pseudo-scientific pretensions, for he scorned the notion 'that in history we can have something more than private points of view of particular historians: that there are "verdicts of history" and that history itself, considered impersonally, has something to say to men'.

Butterfield's central assumption was that assumptions are wrong. He set about showing this in successive works of demolition. In *The Whig Interpretation of History* (1931) he questioned the prevailing approaches to history. In his *Christianity and History* trilogy (1948-51) he questioned, in prophetic manner, the mood of Cold War self-righteousness which made all conflict a conflict of good v. bad, a view of human nature which ignored the Christian view of man. In *The Origins of Modern Science* (1949) he showed how abridgement had led to a propagandist, retrospective view of the seventeenth-century scientific revolution, to placing it as a step towards secularism, toleration, and Bertrand Russell — when it was often the work of pious Christians seeking, in the manner of Bach, to glorify God.

The Peace Tactics of Napoleon, 1806-1808 (1929) tried to show what unabridged history would be like, were such a thing practicable. *George III, Lord North, and the People* (1949) tried to show structures changing in a sociological totality, or more simply that past politics could not be understood in terms of political history, as then conceived. In *George III and the Historians* (1957) he queried Namier's structural approach to eighteenth-century political culture. Namier, Butterfield argued, did not explain how one situation changed into another structure. In other words, structure is not enough; by omitting narrative, one omits truth, by omitting or understating the part played by chance, uncertainties, events, contingencies. Structure may set limits to what can happen (thus trade unionism will not occur in a hunting society), but it can never by itself explain why one course of events took place rather than another.

Here Butterfield plumped for one line of criticism, when another was also needful. When he spoke of the tension between structure and narrative, he could as well have spoken of the tension between structure (in the sense of social and political structure) and values, moral, aesthetic, cultural, religious. For instance, within a European structure which changed relatively little between feudalism and the coming of the railways, cataclysmic variations in values occurred which resist any structural explanation.

Butterfield, in his *Christianity and History* trilogy, and to a lesser extent elsewhere, tried to invent a Christian version of history, or Christian outlook on history. Nobody else has done this. He wanted to make international relations, perhaps his deepest interest, come to terms with Christianity. He presented national policy in terms of sin, temptation, forgiveness. In doing so, he came perilously near to being an apologist for men in power. (How is 'thou shalt not judge' separable from blandness?) In the end, it seemed as though Butterfield's Christianity came to terms with a lightly Christianized power politics: an Anglican position, but one which Dissenters had always sharply questioned. In personal terms, there must be some doubt whether it was not an impish glee in destroying established views, that led him to use the Christian view of man as his main instrument of battle.

One Butterfield doctrine has however hardened into an undue solemnity. This is that hindsight is the historian's cardinal sin. And so it must be, if you wish to know the past as it really was. Yet there are other things one might equally well, in certain contexts, wish to know. With perfect good reason, one may ask, in the context of an outline or introductory course, how great oaks from little acorns grow. This will not enlighten one about the world of the acorn; but it will tell one much about the oak. Provided one is aware what one is doing, hindsight need not be sinful. It all depends on what you are aiming at; and there is certainly more than one possible aim in historical explanation. Here the Butterfield tradition errs towards rigidity.

History as Structure:
Why Namier Matters

Where Butterfield was a lifelong university historian who mattered mainly for books which were not directly historical, Lewis Namier (1888-1960) was a man of many roles who mattered almost entirely for his mainstream historical books. Before he became professor at Manchester at the age of 43, he had spent only two years in university employment. He was proud that he was not a professional or career historian, in an age when history had become a formal career, and yet he has had more influence on professional history in this century than anyone else.

England has had three ghettoes of the mind: the Dissenting, the Catholic, and the Jewish. In the course of the last two centuries, all have been liberated. The liberation of the Dissenters led to their absorption into the national mainstream. The emancipation of Catholicism did not remove their ghetto mentality, and has produced virtually no consequences. The emancipation of the Jewish mind, and its emergence as a non-religious identity separate from Judaism, has transformed modern thought.

Lewis Namier was a European Jew in the age of Hitler. He was the son of a Jewish landowner and lawyer in a part of rural Poland that was then Austrian. His first wife was of uncertain East European extraction, his second Russian, and he spoke with a foreign accent. And he was the world's greatest authority on the reign of George III.

He was an undergraduate at Balliol College, Oxford, in 1908-11. He took U.K. nationality in 1913, and changed his name to Namier by deed poll. There is a certain parallel with the (non-Jewish) novelist Joseph Conrad, also of Polish background.

In 1915-20, while very young, he worked as a Foreign Office specialist on Eastern Europe, being much concerned in the settlement of Polish affairs at Versailles. If his first formative experience was of a stable rural aristocracy, his second was of how states make policy. Later, in the 1930s and 1940s, he was a Zionist activist, and a close associate of the founders of Israel, Weizmann and Ben Gurion. This was his third formative experience.

After a short spell teaching at Oxford, which he found too time-consuming, he went into business in Czechoslovakia so that he had enough to live on while writing the books that he knew were in him.

From 1924 to 1929 he was fully occupied with research. He wrote the books that he had planned to write. When the money ran out, he became a professor at Manchester (1931-53), where A.J.P. Taylor was to be a younger colleague and friend.

Here he ceased to revolutionize history, and became merely an imposing figure. Distracted by Hitler, he became a leading Jewish nationalist working for a state of Israel, and doing history on the side. His idea of 'on the side' was quite considerable for he produced eleven fair-sized volumes of collected essays, as well as studies of the diplomatic origins of the Second War, and an influential re-interpretation of the 1848 Revolutions as 'a revolution of the intellectuals'.

He was a major European historian as well as an English one. His deepest insight was that nationalisms were pathological. They were not noble and libertarian, as English writers had almost invariably thought, but irrational, based on hatred and fantasy, and egged on, or even concocted, by irresponsible and incompetent intelligentsias. Racial and linguistic nationalism was to him an insane obsession, an infection of rootless urban mass politics. If mass politics was thus sinister, then the stable aristocracies of the European ancien regime might have more to be said for them than English liberalism normally allowed. 'Liberty', he wrote, 'is the fruit of slow growth in a stable country ... [it] is in its origin an aristocratic idea'. Namier on modern Europe, and Namier on Hanoverian England, were aspects of a single message.

The Structure of Politics at the Accession of George III (note the novel word 'structure' in the title) came out in 1929. It was Namier's greatest book. *England in the Age of the American Revolution* followed in 1930. It stopped short before the American Revolution had even begun. It was meant to be the start of a multi-volume work, none of which ever came into existence. His work was at once recognized as epoch-making in method, content, and erudition, but especially in method.

In Namier's last phase, he devoted his energies to a massive historical project, the *History of Parliament*, whose very title raised questions about the centrality of parliament which were left for others to answer. Such projects usually languish, but Namier's section of three volumes on 1754-90 was the first in the series to get done. It contained 2,000 biographies of MPs, plus constituency histories, and was virtually complete at his death in 1960. It was well, perhaps superbly well done, considered as work of reference, but it is hard not to see it as a displacement activity for the classic works he never wrote. Such fractures in a writer's life are normal, and Namier's achievement is not seriously diminished by being fragmentary and incomplete.

He is the only historian to give his name to a historical method: Namierization, or the need to understand the total sociological structure of a political nation in its minutest detail of patronage, influence, and kinship, in order to understand its superstructure of ideas, government, culture and events. He was also one of the very few historians to feel the need not just for a historical sociology but for a politically relevant, semi-Freudian psychology of individuals: thus George III was 'a mollusc who never left his shell'. He brought to his writing an experience of diplomacy, business, and the workings of the pre-1914 ancien regime. Namier was as unusual as a man as he was as a historian.

What did Namier see in the eighteenth century? He saw an echo of his stable rural childhood spent in a pre-1914 Polish Austrian manor house. Both were worlds where inequality was a protection against mass politics, and 'the deliberate savagery of the German character' was in abeyance.

Unlike the liberal historians, he found eighteenth-century parliaments, those 'pathetically intent human antheaps', pleasant to contemplate precisely because they were unreformed, precisely because they embodied no principle or higher ideal, precisely because of their attachment to looking after self.

It was principle, after all, not selfish advantage, which over-threw stable, ordered habits of life, and which opened the door to the persecution of Jews. So much the worse for principle, and so much the better for petty selfishness. So much the better, too, for the fairly harmless manoeuvres of the eighteenth-century parliamentarian, seeking a sinecure here, a place in the army, navy, or church for his son, and in return working with the larger self-interests of political faction: all that Old Corruption which had so shocked a liberal morality unable to conceive of real evil.

'Men', he wrote in a famous analogy, 'no more dreamt of a seat in the House of Commons in order to benefit humanity than a child dreamt of a birthday cake in order that others might eat it'. Men did not seek power in order to enact policies, but enacted policies in order to hold power. Namier tried to understand the eighteenth-century parliament in terms of its own time, but the implications for the twentieth century were clear.

One main purpose of Namier's writing was to curtail explanations of eighteenth-century politics based on party, hitherto the established means of analysis, for if principle was a thin disguise for the pursuit of advantage, then parties decomposed into the study of personal connections. This, perhaps the most discussed, and most subsequently modified aspect of Namier's work, is relatively inessential. Certainly, the decade of which he wrote saw party perhaps at its lowest ebb ever; certainly, globules of principle can always just about be found; certainly, at some periods in the eighteenth-century party was a great fact.

Namier's more lasting argument was more moral than technical. He claimed that the unreformed parliament, which he saw as responsive to popular feeling, did not differ in its 'moral and mental dishonesty' from the system of today, or indeed from representative government anywhere. This was true even financially, for it was as normal for eighteenth-century noblemen 'to live on the dole' as it was for all classes to do so today. (As Gladstone said, in unreformed days one bribed individuals; with a democratic electorate, one bribes whole classes.) To Namier, it was the resemblances, not the differences, between today and the eighteenth century that mattered. For him, as for all sensible men, democracy was a legitimizing device for rule by elites, within which individual advantage could decorously be sought. Politics being of the earth earthy, the naive democratic moralism rampant in the 1920s was as much a barrier to understanding the past, as it was a danger in the present.

In essentials, Namier was right. In its own time, politics under George III was as normal as that of any other time and place, and not a cause for liberal hand-wringing and democratic self-congratulation. An aristocracy seeking preferment under a thin disguise of principle, was as morally acceptable as, and indeed less harmful than, twentieth-century mass politics. Namier's historical writing about the eighteenth century must be seen in the light of this implicit comparison, not as mere nostalgic conservatism.

In politics, Namier was non-liberal and anti-liberal rather than conservative in any ordinary English sense. He disliked Labour partly because it supported the Arabs in Palestine. In religion, he was a boyhood Roman Catholic who later became a nominal Anglican, without ever professing Judaism. The central belief of his life was probably a political religion, Zionism, to be achieved by 'a real Jewish militarism' which would free Jews from the character defects imposed upon them by exile.

What did Namier overdo, and what omit? He overrated the centrality of parliament, and the significance of backbenchers, other than as guides to the general political culture. He was wobbly on party. His *History of Parliament*, by its very title, and still more by its monumental contents, implied that parliament mattered to an extent that was not established. He over-Namierized. Such errors in the grand manner are incidental to any large step forward.

More disquieting was his disregard for narrative, event, and contingency. Structure only explains structure; it can never wholly, or even fully, explain the course of events. Indeed, an emphasis on structure can take one away, far away, from what happened. Even the process by which one structure turns into the structure of a later age, is hard to explain purely structurally. In this sense, Namier's new understanding of structure, for such it was, created a barrier to understanding the flow and chanciness of events.

Namier's work on modern Europe remains a source of insight into the pathology of mass politics, the pathology of intelligentsia politics (Hitler, author, artist, architect, in his drivelling way represented the petty intelligentsia in politics, save for his patriotism), the virtues of stable aristocracies, the importance of East European peasant peoples, and the arguments for rabid Germanophobia. Until the demise of the Soviet Empire, there could be no question which of the two Namiers, the student of the antics of English eighteenth-century parliaments, or the student of the destructive forces underlying Eastern and Central Europe, mattered most.

X

Theories about the Past

Theories about the past are extraordinarily few. When historians theorize, it is their methods, not their subject matter, that concern them. Not only do historians avoid theorizing themselves, but they are markedly averse to it in others. Apart from a little shoplifting from sociology, historians are uneasy with theory, and have added little to the world of ideas, or to the vocabulary within which ideas can be given form. Intellectually, history is, like classics, a parasite subject.

There is no justification for this. Recent centuries may have been untypical in their failure to beget historical concepts. Some convergence between history and theory may emerge, or already be happening, even if inchoate, not embodied in masterpieces, and up against the rigidly set mould of educational departmentalism. Such a convergence with theory would not mean renouncing the untidiness of history, nor the primary role of simple factual discovery, but it might mean abandoning the identification of professionalism with divergence from theory.

One theory of history hardly needs discussion. It is that which sees history as the inevitable growth of material well-being. Such growth is true, more so now than in 1900, as it was more true in 1900 than in 1800, and more true in 1800 than in 1700. It is true in the simplest sense of all, that nobody argues to the contrary. We can join Gibbon in the 'pleasing conclusion that every age of the world has increased, and still increases, the real wealth, the happiness, the knowledge, and perhaps the virtue, of the human race'. The economic advance of the world in the last twenty years alone, would equal its progress in the previous century. The Malthusian nightmares so often predicted look more than ever like shroud-waving, as the toilers of India and China join the cheerful throng of progress. The insensitive optimists have proved correct.

This theory has one limitation, equally undisputed: it applies only to the past taken as a whole, not to its parts. It is about getting there in the end, not about what happens on the way. Thus China, after an effervescent youth, had a sorry middle age, while real standards of life for most may have changed little between the Babylonian Ziggurats and the medieval cathedrals, between the cathedrals and the railways. Except to the writer of world history, who can hardly be blind to the triumph of human talent, a theory which adds nothing to our knowledge and understanding of even very large areas of the past is not in practice of much use. This negative verdict fits the mood of a culturally pessimistic, economically lugubrious academic intelligentsia, liable to lose status through material prosperity, and unconnected with the production of wealth. In consequence, no theory of the past is more neglected than the rise from cave man to computer, nor more generally accepted.

Of the theories of the past that were abroad in 1900, few remain. Most were theories of special destinies: half assumptions, half extrapolations, but nevertheless central to explaining the past. At any rate, Protestantism, constitutionalism, industrialism, Marxism, and the central role of Europe all then appeared to offer important explanations.

The special destiny of Protestantism has bitten the dust, all the more so because it fell without an assailant; yet in 1900 it was a plausible explanation of much of history far outside the realm of religion. The special destiny of constitutionalism has mutated into that of liberal democracy. The latter matters only so far as it is not seen to be what it is, whether figleaf of capitalism, figleaf of bureaucracy, or figleaf of manifold new and old elitisms. It was not for this deceptive or persuasive power that constitutionalism, with its huge chronological depth and apparent causative role, seemed a great organizing principle in 1900.

As political and religious explanations of the past receded after 1900, an economic one came to take its place. The idea of industrialism gradually offered itself as a key to the past. Here, far from coming down to earth, we wandered into new pastures of error. In romanticizing the production of goods, and the singularities of English industrialization, a bubble was blown that could only burst as the variousness of the routes to economic modernity came to be understood. Nothing attests more to the semi-religious sensibility of early economic history than its worship of steel. The more insecure the market for steel became, the greater grew its potency as a fetish, far into the 1960s. More generally, the idea of industrialism as human destiny, with its focus on physical objects as the heart of economic and social life, made a wonderfully unreal introduction to a late twentieth-century world experienced through offices and bureaucracies.

The centrality of Europe was once a certainty which history had to explain. This was so no less in 1950 than in 1900. Now it is the marginalization of Europe (even if it is as yet nothing compared to what will follow) which historians need to discuss. There is no clearer case of how a historical theme can turn out to be the opposite of what all educated men expected. This historians, more than most, failed to see; in the 1950s, extra-European history only had a foothold in the syllabus on sufferance. Noticeable exclusions, such as South and South-East Asia, Islam, and Eastern Europe (an 'extra-European' zone newly created by the Cold War), have remained, while the thriving study of Latin America and Africa did little more than reflect their intimacy with the United States and Europe, and their possibilities as an academic soft option.

Explanatory theories of the past are thus not very reliable, even within periods of one or two generations. In comparison with these misconceptions, the theory of inexorable material progress has a monumental unassailability. By comparison with the gods that have failed this century, Marx and Toynbee, alone among individual writers, merit much attention.

Karl Marx (1818-83) was not a historian. He was however a great European intellectual who thought historically. He did so in several ways. In the first place, he wrote a limited amount of excellent, undogmatic contemporary history. Secondly, his economics was broadly historical in conception. It sought to explain not only how capitalism worked, and in what direction it was moving, but why it had come to be there in the first place. Thirdly, he held that all history was the history of class conflict, which in turn arose from the conditions of production of the time, and their incompatibility with the existing power structure. This turned history 'bottom up' with a vengeance, and on the whole it has stayed that way. The doctrine that Marx called materialism, meaning that the superstructure (art, religion, high politics) was the outcome of material conditions, was not a crude assertion that 'what matters is matter, and I don't mind about mind'. Again, materialism, as Marx used the word, meant something wider than technological determinism. It meant the primacy of social exist- ence, almost of life as we find it – a doctrine so broad that it is often hard for anyone, whatever their politics, to disagree with it. Marx's social materialism, subtly used, as he in fact used it, was an addition to understanding, more akin to common sense than to political commitment. Crassly used, in other hands, it denied the complexity of things, reduced civilization to banalities, and was a great step backward.

What Marx really knew about was the nineteenth century. His ideas on class conflict before that time were never fully worked out. They should be seen, not as errors, but perhaps more as methodo- logical imperatives, urging others not to omit class from their research. Not that class was Marx's invention; he used, and devel- oped, the common terminology of his day, giving it a deeper, more historical meaning. He gave to the working class a messianic role, extrapolating here from the part that he thought that the bourgeoi- sie had played in the transition from feudalism to capitalism. His lavish idealization of the bourgeoisie, his own class, and its sup- posed dynamic, creative role in history raises the biggest question of all.

Marx's theory of class is valuable as a hard-minded reminder of the inexorable nature of one particular kind of antagonism, and perhaps too for its insistence on the inexorability of things gener- ally. As a potential explanation, it is a useful tool to have to hand; class struggle should be looked for everywhere, not least within the left itself, even if Marx, being much more an economist than a sociologist, left class undefined. It is only when the inexorability of class is used to hide other aspects of inexorability in history that it becomes a dogmatism. He stressed, rightly, the inescapability of conflict, but not its infinite mutability. Thus, for instance, he underplayed the role of war, physical force, taxation, bureaucracy, dictatorship, terrorism, inflation, and totalitarianism. By concentrating on the everyday victimhood of the poor, he made the world sound pleasanter than it was in fact to be in the twentieth century. In this he was truly Victorian, truly of his own time – as, according to his own theory, he could not but be. He had no insight into the central political issue in modern society: the inexorable conflicts over the allocation of resources within the collectivist state, for Marx lived in the most lightly taxed, least collectivist society in history. He is the Mr Gladstone of historical thought, an awesomely justice-loving voice from a vanished individualist world.

There have been many Marxes. In the revolutionary 1840s, Marx was revolutionary. In maturity, in the non-revolutionary second half of the century, he was non-revolutionary except on a very long time scale. (Thus he was not an active Communist, did not try to found a British Communist Party, and was closest to the respectable parliamentarianism of the Social Democrats in Germany.)

The real Marx, a mid-Victorian writer manqué, a Balzac (his favourite author) rather than a Darwin, a disorganized humanist thinker and perpetual student, was turned by the late Victorians into a late Victorian scientist, exuding rigid laws. Then, after 1917, the Russians turned this essentially libertarian rebel and individualist into an efficient Leninist social engineer. The liberated 1960s produced a blue-jeaned Marx, eternally 25, concerned with religion, philosophy and alienation, in rebellion against his later self, and against later officious attempts to turn Marxism into a universal science. Each generation invents its own Marx.

Beyond doubt, Marx invested more energy on economics than anything else, and more hope on the working class than on anyone else. Yet the economics are the one almost universally disregarded part of his work, the one part not to catch the eye and heart of posterity; while late twentieth-century Marxism has been the icon of student youth, of Western intelligentsias generally, and of Third World modernizers – all privileged groups, all unconnected with workers. Nevertheless, Marxism has known two rebirths, in the

Thirties and in the Sixties, in the latter case as a world-wide vehicle for inter-generational conflict. To say that there will be no third renaissance would be bold indeed.

In Marx we find a grand unfolding of the pattern of history, with the conditions of production as a prime element. In Marx's successor and opponent, Max Weber, there is a grand unfolding in the institutions and political culture of society (even if the conditions of production do not move in step). Neither Marx nor Weber negates in principle the possibility of a further grand unfolding on a spiritual level (whether of Reason or of Love, as in Hegel or Teilhard de Chardin respectively), unless it is claimed, as it usually is, that this inner spiritual momentum in history means that there is no other pattern or structure. When the partisan intentions of the original theorists are taken away, then many different grand patterns, concurrently operative over long periods, might be a possibility. At any rate, the main obstacle to theories of the past is not the existence of conflicting rival theories.

Toynbee is little discussed now. He is easily dismissed as a Cold War phenomenon of the Fifties, the bourgeois-religious alternative to Marxism. However, to judge him either by his adherents or his personal context is unproductive. Toynbee was right where he was likely to be right.

Toynbee, a classicist and student of the ancient Near East, found history to be cyclical. In the ancient Near East, more than anywhere else, cyclical it was. Moreover, Toynbee dealt by preference with the more cyclical elements in history. He dealt with the highly significant activity of the relatively few – those who maintained high culture and religious activity. It was here, among priests rather than peasants, that discontinuities were inherently most likely. Whether discontinuity equals cyclicality, or implies recurrence of similar entities, is another matter. But, in the end, Toynbee's strengths and weaknesses coincide. The objection commonly made, that he deals with only that very small part of human activity which he chooses to call civilization, points to his strength. The cultural cycles he is interested in, have little to do with power, wealth, technique, social order, organization, or size of political units. By limiting what he specially deals with, Toynbee approaches the truistic, even if he gave his perceptions about

antiquity a rashly wide extension into modern times, provoking a
hornets' nest of criticism.

Toynbee was sociological where one would not have expected
him to be, in his sense of the rotation of elites (and the unimpor-
tance of other ranks). He gave religion a place in the
understanding of the past that all pre-Enlightenment civilizations
would have given it, and which post-Enlightenment writers were
not meant to give it.

Chronologically, he stepped outside the parochialism of the last
three millennia, and geographically, he presented the centrality,
first of the Mediterranean, then of Europe, as parentheses in
human history. He erased the gap between BC and AD, albeit more
portentously and religiosely than his vastly different forerunner
H.G. Wells had done. Whether the 21 civilizations he identified
and described were the proper units of study that he thought,
whether they were each comparable with the others, and whether
they could yield general conclusions about 'challenge and response'
was in large part obscured by the generous helpings of embarrassing crankiness which filled his ten huge volumes, the sharp enmity
of professional historians whose intellectual capital lay in a post-
BC world, and Toynbee's hopes of a world state and world religion.
(If by a world religion one means liberal democracy, and by a world
state Ronald Reagan's ending of the Cold War, then Toynbee was
nearer the mark than he would have cared to realize.)

Toynbee said of the ten huge volumes of *A Study of History*:
'Human beings awake to consciousness to find themselves in
chaos. They then try to impose order on this chaos in order to make
life endurable. We cannot verify whether the chart that we make
of the mysterious universe corresponds to the elusive reality, but
in order to live we have to make this chart, realizing it is an act of
faith which is also an act of self-preservation.'

Compared to such dogmatisms as H.A.L. Fisher's famous 'History is one damned thing after another', such honest doubt is the
best justification of theories of the past. They are little use, but one
has to have them, and those who think that they are free of them,
will be most rigidly bound to some body of unconscious assumptions. Charts are instruments of navigation.

The Evolution of Historical Study: Bede to Acton

The history of historical writing has usually been Whig history. Like all such, it sees the present as better than the past. It is informed by a deep belief that historical study has gradually improved: that the centuries laboured, in order to give birth to current professional or academic history. There is something in this, though with important exceptions.

Most medieval historians were not good historians. Some were. For their weaknesses, there were good reasons. They wrote in the shadow of the supremacy of abstract thought. Compared with theology and philosophy, history was but lowly. As monks, they were inevitably out of London, out of court, not directly in touch with the great world (though, since monasteries served as hotels, they encountered more men of note than do most modern academics). They did not meet other historians. They were credulous about miracles, and they saw God as directly intervening in everyday events. They were uncritical of their often dubious or forged sources. Being clergy, their standards were narrowly clerical; good kings were those good to the church, as to modern academics good prime ministers are those who are good to universities. They had no sense of anachronism, and thought the past was in essentials like the present, or the present with but a different cast. Sometimes, not just from laziness, they were liable to use classical models such as Suetonius almost word for word, without acknowledgment and in all innocence. We rarely know what medieval kings actually looked like. There were chroniclers, writers of annals rather than authors of books; though on the other hand annals had the reliability attaching to contemporaneous evidence.

History was a monastic relaxation, not a university subject. It did not develop academically in the middle ages, because it was never seen as academic. It was not taught to the young. It lay outside the ferment of medieval thought and high culture. Hence between the twelfth and the fifteenth centuries there was no general improvement. There was perhaps some decline in quality, related to a general decline in English monasticism itself in its last centuries. The history of historical study in the middle ages was not a history of progress. Some of the best history, indeed, came from the eleventh and twelfth centuries, when true historians such as William of Malmesbury (1090-1143), William of Newburgh (1136-1201) and Eadmer (1060-1128), the Saxon biographer of Anselm, wrote politically acute studies of the post-Norman period, while in the thirteenth century Matthew Paris, monk of St Albans, a monastery much frequented by travellers to and from London, transcended the genre of contemporary chronicle: Henry III sought him for conversation, and some speak of such men as originators of the political interview. But to gain a flavour of medieval history at its best and worst, we must turn to the two best-sellers, Bede (160 copies extant) and Geoffrey of Monmouth (200 copies extant, with important borrowings in nominally independent texts).

Bede (672-735), a Northumbrian monk who never left Northumbria, transcended his time. His masterpiece, the *Ecclesiastical History of the English People*, stated its sources, named its authorities, sought out and used primary sources, some from Canterbury, one from Rome, invented dating by AD and BC instead of by regnal years, wove a rich web of meaning, and gently ground an axe. In all this he was as modern as the moderns; but whereas once it was the precocity of his technique which most excited applause, today it is his art in going beyond technique, his construction of a personal vision of events, which reaches us across the centuries.

Bad history perhaps made a greater mark on medieval culture than good. Its greatest practitioner was Geoffrey of Monmouth (1100-1154), a poorly educated Welshman, willing to try his hand at anything, whose eventual reward was the see of St Asaph. His main work, the *Historia Regum Britanniae*, mixed entertainment, flattery, and national sentiment. It absorbed Celtic country tales, folk myths, and a smattering of classical learning, and in particular made Arthur a central literary figure. (Geoffrey also wrote a life of Merlin for good measure.)

Geoffrey's historical value was nil, his popularity enormous, and his influence on subsequent writers great. Despite his unlimited garrulity, and his having been scornfully dismissed by other historians in his own lifetime, his fictions retained some authority until the early seventeenth century. His creations – Lear, Sabrina, (Old King) Cole – took on a life of their own, and his invention of 100 British kings in order to trace a British descent from the ancient world and from the princes of Troy provoked little objection. His function was to provide a new Anglo-Norman nation with blue blood and a pedigree, something that required exceptionally bad history. But for Geoffrey and the illusory world he created, medieval historical writing might more readily have been credited with the reputation for a patchy if limited respectability that it deserves.

Medieval historical study was in fact becalmed. It developed neither in technique nor in broad historical habits of thought. It had however one little remarked strength. It was, for those writing it, mostly contemporary or modern history. It dealt with matters nearer to its own present, than the central traditions of historical writing were to do after 1500. This was so of necessity, but it is important that it was so: the medieval writers point a finger of reproach at our practice. Twelfth-century historians of the twelfth century get nearer the bone than do histories of the nineteenth century written in the nineteenth century.

In the Tudor and Stuart periods historical study changed out of all recognition. It would be wrong however to see this efflorescence, for such it was, as primarily a change in the direction of the present.

History was no longer monastic, for the monasteries had been dissolved. It was in English, not Latin. It was lay rather than clerical. It reflected the preoccupations of lawyers and an educated gentry. It was not undertaken for the profits of authorship; not until the eighteenth century, with Hume and Gibbon, did history become a source of income. Indeed, as history grew in learning, it lost its entertainment value. Universities did not teach history, and there were no historians in English universities; but unlike in medieval times, this disconnection from universities was perhaps a strength, for they were no longer the great generator of intellectual excitement. History now gained a certain standing, despite its not playing any specific part in educating the young, because it lay at the heart of public debate, legal, religious, and political.

History was no longer miraculous. By 1600 God had become a president, not a chief executive. This enthronement did not diminish the framework of salvation, but historians, now unable to make God the dogsbody responsible for everyday causation, had to reflect more deeply on the causes of things. This was an uncomfortable position. A secular branch of knowledge in a society built round religion, touching on the rawest nerves of that society, overshadowed by the prestige of classics in education and letters, unsupported by any great systematizers like Bacon or Newton, needed to build a safe institutional base on the margins of the polity.

This it did fairly well. Of the necessities of history, in the form of libraries, societies, and awareness of the views of other scholars, all were present save the existence of a learned journal. (The *Philosophical Transactions of the Royal Society*, the first scientific journal, commenced in 1665; the first U.K. historical journal, the *English Historical Review*, began in 1886.) The records of the English medieval monarchy, still unsorted and stored in wretched condition all over London, were only slowly retrieved from the brink of destruction by the exertions of patrons of scholarship in the House of Lords. Against all odds, the public records survived; and on them, more than on any other body of evidence, the progress of historical understanding depended.

Tudor history was a history of national pride, of a growing sense of Englishness, of a love of survivals from the past, but its first and perhaps weightiest practitioner, Polydore Vergil (1470-1555), an Italian humanist, had been both a papal courtier and secretary to an Italian duke, before he became the first modern English historian. Commissioned by Henry VII in 1505, in 1534 he gave Henry VIII a *History of England* in 26 books, going down to 1509. Though his work was still full of portents and omens, it was nevertheless a work of research based on wide use of sources, and also conveyed a sense that the past was different – the true historical sense. It deservedly became a standard work, the first of its kind.

Polydore Vergil exemplified what Tudor historians were not usually like. In the main, they recorded, preserved, collected, rather than analysed. They held it no shame to be called antiquaries, a term hinting at miscellaneous curiosity, rather than historians. Indeed, with their foundation of the Society of Antiquaries in 1572, one can for the first time say that a historian was someone who knew other historians. They were, more than anything, strongly topographical. (The best known of early mapmakers, Speed, also wrote a *History of England*.) Inspired by safer travel, royal interest, and a growing sense of national pride, the Tudor topographers were the first men to see England with thinking eyes.

From topography it was only a step to archaeology. It was under Elizabeth that the 'prehistory of prehistory' began. We know what Stonehenge looked like in Tudor times. Even if archaeology remained above ground, it pushed back the frontiers of time. So too did the first study of Anglo-Saxon, until then a lost tongue; among a select few, unpublished word lists began to circulate, opening the door to a forgotten culture. Megalithic and monastic merged in something quite new, a sense of a remote, unfamiliar, rapidly vanishing past.

John Leland (1506-62) was the first antiquary. Librarian to Henry VIII, a royal chaplain, a keen Protestant, and the first and last King's Antiquary (1533-), he was required to make a search for English antiquities in all cathedrals, abbeys, and colleges. His tour of England (1536-42), a one-man cultural Domesday, left copious notes, published not in his own day, but preserved by private collectors, and finally printed as his *Itinerary* (1710) and *Collectanea* (1715).

After Leland, the topographical tradition divided, with an essential unity, into national and local; national, as in the *Britannia* of William Camden (1551-1623), master, then headmaster, of Westminster School, and local, as in the work of William Lambarde (1536-1601), author of the *Perambulation of Kent* (1574), the first county history in a genre that was to flourish greatly, culminating perhaps in Dugdale's *Warwickshire*. Camden's *Britannia* (1586), a towering work frequently revised and reprinted, combined extensive fieldwork and the use of records to an extent not previously known, making him a model for the succeeding generation.

History in Tudor times, unlike in the middle ages, was rarely contemporary history, perhaps for reasons of prudence. The monastic chroniclers left no successors, or only the palest imitations. There was some biography, such as Cavendish's *Wolsey* and Roper's *More*, both based on personal intimacy and showing psychological acuteness; but very little. Works of high literary ambition, like Sir Walter Raleigh's *History of the World* (1614) which reached only as far as the first century BC and gave much thought to the location of the Garden of Eden, were less modern than those of humbler men writing in humble topographical vein.

The topographers apart, it is perhaps the collectors, not the writers, who laid the basis for the great tradition of English medieval studies, already far advanced in the seventeenth century, and renewed after a lapse of over a century in the third quarter of the nineteenth century, almost as if no space had intervened.

The great collectors deserve a note. The first, Matthew Parker (1504-75), Elizabeth's first archbishop of Canterbury, hoped that history would prove him right, by showing that the Church of England was of great antiquity, with Roman control a mere modern usurpation. As the first married archbishop, he also sought to show that clerical marriages were originally permitted. He published the first printed book in Anglo-Saxon, a civilization not seriously explored until the next century. His collection, at Corpus Christi College, Cambridge, survives intact.

Sir Robert Cotton (1571-1631), founder of the Cottonian Library, was the greatest of private collectors. The eldest son of a rich squire, he devoted his London house to his passion for collecting. Favoured by James I, the only intellectual English monarch, it became an informal club for the learned. The Antiquarian Society met at Cotton House; Camden and others left it their papers. For three generations the library remained in the family, passing from father to son but having a national status and being freely used by scholars. Under Anne the family presented it to the nation, who looked after it badly. In 1731 fire did great damage; of 958 manuscripts, 114 were totally, and 98 partially destroyed. Only in 1753, with the foundation of the British Museum, did the Cottonian Library reach safety.

Sir Thomas Bodley (1545-1613), a successful Elizabethan diplomatist, made perhaps the most efficacious academic bequest ever when he presented the Bodleian Library, England's first public library, to the University of Oxford (whose medieval library had fallen into ruin). With Bodley as the driving force, the library opened in 1602, and its stature was soon enhanced when in 1610 the Stationers' Company (of London) agreed that a copy of each book published should be made available free to the Library. Between them, Parker, Cotton, and Bodley assembled what was needful for historians, and preserved it for a post-monastic world.

Under the Stuarts history came of age. It was learned history, not literary history. It was the product of systematic and laborious research into documents. It embodied an ideal of scholarship as a vocation. It tended to the colossal. If little read now, that is partly because it was already too advanced for non-specialists in its own time, partly because it excelled in putting into print the materials for its own supersession. The work of distinctive individuals, in sum and in retrospect it amounts to a great collective enterprise, similar to that involved in the scientific revolution of the seventeenth century.

There were exceptions to the rule of learning. There were works of high literary quality. Never have politicians written so well about politics (though they wrote as politicians as well as historians). Such subtle observers of the texture of near-contemporary high politics as Clarendon, Halifax, Dryden, and Burnet had no medieval parallel, for they wrote from their experience as participants. They lacked successors. Less subtle, but more influential, was the Protestant polemical tradition, from Foxe's *Martyres* (1563), to the accounts of the 1641 massacres in Ulster, to the 'Black Legend' of the Spanish Inquisition. All served as historical underpinnings of protestantism. All established that the essence of catholicism was cruelty; indeed the very idea of cruelty had anti-Romish connotations. No 'fact' has sunk more deeply into the English mind.

Biography, as a genre, had barely begun, and one might go as far as to say that at no period has it been either an important impetus to research, or an important form of research. 'History' in the seventeenth century meant above all English medieval history, and constitutional and legal history (as opposed to the history of political events) at that. Medieval, and English medieval, it necessarily had to be, if it was to be based on large bodies of documentary evidence: evidence handled in huge bulk, with complete authority, and with an insight enviable today.

On the medieval constitution so much then seemed to turn. The Stuart scholar, in his search for a purer scholarship, was also throwing light on the most vexed questions of his own time. In church and state, the great issues were historical. In law, the great issues were historical. Magna Carta perhaps best symbolized the kind of battleground on which the search for a myth of the English past took place. Since medieval studies gave greater support to authority and Rome than to popular liberties and the idea of a national church, medievalists tended to be Royalists and sometimes catholics. Medievalism showed the Stuart case to be broadly right: another reason for its sharp decline once the Stuarts had gone.

It was an age of heroes. William Dugdale (1605-86), country gentleman and herald, was only the greatest of a type. He wrote the *Monasticon* (3 vols, 1655-73), a vast mass of original material on the monastic history of England. As a matter of local patriotism, he wrote *The Antiquities of Warwickshire* (1656), a masterpiece of county history, a genre which for four centuries has been as richly English as choral music. He compiled the *Baronage*, the first genealogical study of the Norman feudal families; and again, such 'stud books' of an enduring upper class came to be a remarkable branch of learning, culminating in G.E. Cokayne's *Complete Peerage* and Burke's *Landed Gentry*. Dugdale was also father of nineteen children. Any one of these feats would make a modern reputation.

Grubbing in medieval records meant an intimate involvement with the great collections. There was no British Museum; the Public Records, scattered across London, took second place to the Cottonian Library, the Bodleian, and later the Harleian, maintained by Robert Harley, Earl of Oxford. All had cataloguers and librarians, some great scholars: a new form of employment for the learned. Much turned on paternalism. Humfrey Wanley (1672-1726), once a Coventry draper's assistant, later Harley's librarian and the greatest Anglo-Saxon scholar, was sent to Oxford by his bishop. Thomas Hearne (1678-1735), a poor boy, then an omniscient keeper at the Bodleian and the man who put Leland into print, was sent to Oxford by the local gentry. George Hickes (1642-1715), whose *Thesaurus* of 1703 first set out the grammar of all the Germanic medieval languages, was a farmer's boy. One did not have to be a gentleman-scholar like Dugdale to do great things. History in the seventeenth century was the common effort of a whole society: patrons, collectors, institutions, gentry, divines, librarians, cataloguers, archivists, printers, poor scholars with a manifest vocation, and even a king, James I, himself an early visitor to the Bodleian Library.

History in the eighteenth century both went into decline and flourished as never before. It became a source of fame, as with Edward Gibbon (1737-94). It became a source of income, as with David Hume (1711-76). It propagated the ideas of the Enlightenment, as with Voltaire (1694-1778). It enhanced its position as a school of political wisdom for members of the ruling class, second only in esteem to classics. Above all, the eighteenth century saw the beginnings of the primacy of literary history, history conceived as literature, as a work of art. Literary history had always existed; what was new was its primacy, continuing through the first half of the nineteenth century, at the expense of some decline in pure scholarship.

The case of Gibbon deserves more notice. A country gentleman, an M.P., and a son of an M.P., he more than anyone established the gentlemanliness of history, even, perhaps, in his bachelor's indecencies and profanities. In all but genius he marked a departure from the true line of growth in the subject, a decline from its previous peak. He used no unprinted archives; his library was his own home. Did he discover anything not previously known? Did he really, as the phrase goes, 'do research'? Perhaps not; not, that is, as we understand research today, but also as his late seventeenth– and early eighteenth century predecessors understood it. No great historian so visibly stood on other men's shoulders nor so honestly acknowledged his dependence. Gibbon was learned, but more, he was philosophy reflecting upon learning. None so clearly pointed the wrong way forward. By his choice of subject, no less than by his method, he pointed to the supremacy of a reviving classical scholarship, and away from the slumbering archives of the medieval states of Europe.

Up to 1720, the study of archives, which in England meant necessarily the archives of the English medieval monarchy, had proved and was proving astonishingly fruitful. About 1720, this heroic phase ended. The questions at the heart of public affairs – monarchy, parliament, law, church – no longer required specifically historical answers. In the seventeenth century, archival research could hope to settle the burning issues of the day. After 1720, the burning issues not only became pale embers, but thought took a more abstract turn. Worse than that, what the English medievalists unearthed was far too favourable to Crown and Rome for comfort, and lent no support to myths of the inborn freedom of the English people and the ancient independence of their Church.

This development coincided with the entry of history, at long last, into the English universities. The endowment of university chairs of history was an enlightened mark of royal esteem, but unfortunately it did not make any difference. Historians, being appointed by ministers, were enmeshed in the Hanoverian patronage system. More than a few professors of history were not historians at all. There were no English university historians of note between 1730 and 1860. In any case, the eighteenth century was a bad century for English universities. University history meant paying professors not to write, or even teach, history. It was only a century or more later that this institutional foothold provided a basis for academic history.

By 1970 there were 13,000 professional academic historians in the United States alone, writing, if they did, chiefly for colleagues, and teaching university students. A century earlier, one could barely glimpse the beginnings of the process that led to this state of affairs, except perhaps in Germany. Perhaps the number of active historians of note was no greater in 1870, than in 1170, 1270, 1370, or 1670; certainly, if the greatly increased population is taken into account. In England, university history began in the third quarter of the nineteenth century.

It did not grow out of such epic works of synthesis as Macaulay's *History of England*, Carlyle's *French Revolution* (1837), Arnold's *Rome* (1838-43), Grote's *Greece* (1846-56), James Mill's *History of British India* (1818), Milman's *History of the Jews* (1830), Finlay's *History of Greece from its Conquest by the Romans to the Present Time* (1877), H.T. Buckle's *History of Civilisation* (1857-61), or Lord Acton's unwritten *History of Liberty*. Such writers were not based in universities, were not deeply concerned with archival scholarship, did not have and did not want a historical journal, and did not see, or want to see, historians as a profession. Their allegiance was to literature, and to the understanding of an educated reading public. In 1850, their conception of history appeared unassailable. They were history, and there seemed no reason why they and their like should not continue so for ever.

Beneath the surface, the Victorians were at work, and in another direction. The Public Record Office, founded in 1838, moved to its new building in Chancery Lane in 1866: a classic case of an administrative backwater undergoing a Victorian spring cleaning. The Camden Society (from 1838), the Early English Texts Society (from 1864), and the Royal Commission on Historical Manuscripts (from 1869) formed external buttresses to scholarship. These institutional developments, though useful, and though far removed from the world of Gibbon, Macaulay, and Carlyle, did not particularly help history to gatecrash the universities, where its absence had so long gone unlamented; the Royal Historical Society, for instance, though founded in 1868, was not presided over by an academic until 1901.

William Stubbs (1825-1901) did more than anyone to found history as a mainstream university subject. Born the son of a solicitor in the quiet Yorkshire country town of Knaresborough, whose grammar school he attended, he went to Oxford as a sizar, a category of student not far removed in status from college servant. While serving as a conscientious country vicar in Essex (where he taught Swinburne) he made himself the most learned medievalist in the country. In 1866, in what was partly a characteristic act of ancien regime preferment, Lord Derby, then Tory premier, offered Stubbs, a Tory high churchman, the Regius Chair of History at Oxford, the first time it had gone to a great working scholar. Doubtless some such development would have occurred sooner or later, whether from imitation of the German universities, or from the awakening and numerical expansion of the public schools and of Oxford and Cambridge. The former university established a separate history degree in 1871, the latter in 1873. For all that, a chasm separated Stubbs from all his predecessors at either university.

Between 1866 and 1884, when he became a bishop, Stubbs inspired the rapidly expanding Oxford history school, creating history as a student degree subject founded on primary sources. His *Select Charters* (1870), being in the original Latin, did more than any other single book to establish the difficulty, and hence academic respectability, of his subject at undergraduate level; Stubbs was the father of the time-honoured examination 'gobbet' – which, despite its slight connotation of pedantry when a Victorian innovation, has lately passed into school examinations as a touchstone of educational enlightenment. Stubbs was himself amazingly productive. His work in putting fifteen large volumes of medieval chronicles into print was only nominally that of an editor, for the introduction to each was itself a weighty piece of research.

Apart from being a prodigy of industry, Stubbs wrote a majestic work of synthesis, the *Constitutional History* (1873-8) whose three volumes end in 1485. His critics variously regard him as wrong (a characteristic of first attempts at synthesis), or as putting the seal of historical self-approval, with hindsight, on the constitutionalism and parliamentarianism of Victorian England. They damn him, in particular, for not being F.W. Maitland (1850-1907), a medievalist's medievalist, a visibly cleverer man, and for most of the twentieth century the only historian to be a cult figure among his kind. Still, with Maitland history took a wrong turning, however cleverly, in the direction of failure to grasp political motive, and not in the medieval period only.

There were other differences. Whereas Stubbs was a Tory parson and Christian moralist, Maitland was an agnostic liberal, a temper of mind more congenial to most whose duty it was to compare the two. Such things count. In the end, however, it is not a comparison of like with like; Maitland left an essentially personal reputation, Stubbs transformed the way in which history was practised. The conscientious reactionary parson was far the more revolutionary figure.

It was not as simple as that. It rarely is. There are always secondary figures. College tutors, if not in harmony with Stubbs, provided essential ballast. Free-wheeling literary historians were far from extinct. Stubbs himself was succeeded in the Oxford chair by E.A. Freeman (1873-92), not a university teacher, though remorselessly learned (as the excerpts from him in *Alice in Wonderland* show), and one of the sharpest polemicists of the day. At Cambridge, the chair of history was long held (1869-95) by Sir John Seeley (1834-95), who was happiest with general works of ideas such as *Ecce Homo*, a mildly modernizing portrayal of Christ, and *The Expansion of England*, a reflection upon imperial destiny.

Deviance from the line laid down by Stubbs perhaps went further in the *Short History of the English People* (1874) by J.R. Green, a parson, working outside university life, whose preference was for 'common things' over 'great events'. Green wanted to found social history, but did not; Seeley, under the slogan 'history is past politics', wanted a broad political history. Stubbs wanted a constitutional history, and made sure he got it; the link between the workings of the constitution and the workings of Christian morality he failed to get.

History, or university history, long had fortune on its side. The social sciences hardly existed, except for economics, and that was to remain educationally marginal until between the wars. Modern languages were ill thought of. English, above all, was not a subject. It was the common inheritance of educated men. The idea that it might be a subject, first mooted in the 1880s, gained little hold until after 1945. History throve because of lack of competition, more than for any other single reason.

Like English later, it was seen as containing elements of moral uplift, as well as being the line of educational least resistance. Though not easy, it was easier than the main alternative, classics. Its educational base expanded, with the expansion of the Victorian public schools, few of whose products were fit meat for the science laboratory. History gained, too, from its associations with state-craft, at a time when political society by general consent constituted the highest element in polite society. Had history not existed, it would have been necessary, by 1900, to invent a similar subject to much the same formula. The pursuit of truth had its place, to be sure, but there were great social forces at work as well.

Victorian history ended with high hopes, exemplified by Lord Acton's *Cambridge Modern History*, and by the *English Historical Review*, founded in 1886. Mandell Creighton (1843-1901), the editor of the *Review* from its foundation to 1891, was a parson who became, like Stubbs, a bishop. The son of a Carlisle draper, Creighton was educated, like Stubbs, at a minor northern grammar school and Oxford, going on to do, in lesser degree, for European history what Stubbs had done for English medieval history. It was Creighton's *History of the Papacy 1378-1527* (5 vols, 1882) which raised the question of moral judgments in history that so exercised Acton, embroiling him in strenuous dispute with Creighton. It was also the book that Acton ought to have written.

Lord Acton (1834-1902), Regius professor at Cambridge from 1895, mattered because he was wrong. There were several Actons. As a moralist, he held that it was 'the office of historical science to maintain morality as the sole criterion'. Though this may look like a statement about morality, it is really a statement about sociology and evidence. That is, it assumes that truth will out; and it assumes that there will long be a stable and free educated class able to care about the truth when it does come out. The idea that it mattered, in the long run, whom history praised and whom it damned, depended very much on society remaining forever as Acton knew it: a wild assumption.

Acton was just as wrong about historical objectivity. Not himself a professional historian, it fell to him to show, entirely contrary to his own intentions, the limitations of the new professional objectivity in history. Mere fairness and scholarliness, even in the hands of Acton, a man of European vision, could not be made to yield finality. The nineteenth-century transformation of history raised more questions than it answered. The stately edifice of Acton's posthumous *Cambridge Modern History* (1902-10) aimed at a synthesis where one could no longer tell 'where a Frenchman had laid down his pen, and where a German had picked it up'.

Perhaps something like that was achieved, where purely national and religious quarrels were concerned. If so, it only made the remaining difficulties more apparent. In particular, Acton had to organize the material of his contributors by themes, periods, and problems. Such choices contained an irreducible element of subjectivity and interpretation, whether that of the editor or of his age. Periodization, the only area where history approaches conceptual self-sufficiency, turned out to be quite as perilous, quite as full of rigidity and bias, as any quarrel of French and Germans. Twentieth-century historical writing, which began with Acton's heroic attempt at a universal synthesis, has gone on to see the crumbling of the structure which Acton built and nowhere more so than in his preferred arena of Renaissance and Reformation.

XII

Economic History

That modern schools of history are incurably miscellaneous, and lack any general tendency, does not mean that they are dainty creatures of fashion, here today and gone tomorrow. Nobody would say that economic history, for instance, was a creature of fashion, a creation of the post-1945 generation when its influence reached its height. On the contrary, its roots lie deep in the nineteenth century. Its teachings are authoritative. It has its own distinctive technology. And, unlike general history (for its unlikeness is often its chief feature), it has set much store by its claim to be a social science – perhaps one rather closer to the earthy realities of economic life than much of economics itself.

Before 1914, economic history was not quite part of the historical establishment. There was no distinct chair in the subject until 1892, when Harvard created one for the Oxford scholar W.J. Ashley (1860-1927). There was no full-time lecturer in economic history at an English university until 1904. It featured only peripherally in the new history degrees set up at Oxford and Cambridge in the 1870s. It was not that it was entirely new. Perhaps it began with the Glasgow professor Adam Smith (1723-90), whose *Wealth of Nations* (1776) used history to draw supra-historical lessons. 'There is scarcely a page of *The Wealth of Nations*', wrote Unwin, 'where history and theory are sundered from each other.' It first flourished in Germany from around the mid-nineteenth century, its great names being Roscher and Schmoller. There it reflected the struggle for an economic national identity, and often enough for protectionism, or at least a rejection of the supposedly purely logical and non-historical 'truth' of free trade. From the German belief in the primacy of historical experience in the making and understanding of law, represented by the school of the great jurist Savigny, to a belief in the primacy of experience in economics, was but a step.

For free trade nations like England, however, economic history was hardly necessary. For them, pure reason, not historical experience, guided policy, and it had proved entirely adequate; they had no need of an 'alternative' economics. German prowess in economic history was not therefore calculated to impress England, where indeed it was but little known; and it was internal influences, not imitation, which first, and for long, made England turn to economic history.

Economic history began seriously in Britain when the British economy began to look problematical. Between the collapse of the rural economy in 1879, and the first Dock Strike of 1888, economic history emerged. Its agenda was influenced by the crisis in English agriculture, industrial decline related to German and American competition, and the question of urban poverty. Of course, there had always been economic anxieties; but the eighteenth-century concern with commercial history, and the early Victorian preoccupation with the inexplicable volatility of the business cycle, now took second place. Economic history was distinctly of its own time: a late Victorian attempt to answer late Victorian problems.

As such, it oozed bias, political, social, religious. It looked to, and drew on, the new secular faiths: late Victorian socialism, late Victorian imperialism, Edwardian new liberalism. It was almost always collectivist; on that at least socialist and protectionist readily agreed. It put the interests of Britain, or the British worker, before that of the smooth working of global free trade capitalism.

If economic history was partly inspired by rejection of free trade economics, it was also part of the *fin de siècle* rediscovery of the state. For many, a commitment to economic history involved upheaval, a sense of self-discovery or conversion, rather than a staid or orderly academic progression. Significantly, it was not until 1958 that a holder of a British chair in the subject had studied it for his undergraduate degree; economic historians always began by being something else.

There were of course politically engaged liberals in economic history, some of them, like Unwin and T.S. Ashton at Manchester, and Thorold Rogers, the historian of prices, important figures in its story; but their fierce engagement arose from a sense of dispossession by the collectivist tide. Intervention versus non-intervention, big state versus little state, protection versus free trade: this was the essential axis of debate, and it gave the first generation of economic historians a sense of public consequence which subsequent generations found it hard to maintain.

Purely party debate, in the sense of Liberals v. Conservatives, or even Left v. Right, or even debate about capitalism, its merits and direction, played little part. By the time leading economic historians got to grips with capitalism, indeed, in the generation after 1945, it was a rather different kind of capitalism that they had to consider: for capitalism had become corporatism, a form of intelligent, rational managerialism not unlike that preached by early collectivists. Nowhere was this tendency to oligopoly more marked than in mid-twentieth-century Britain, with its exceptionally high degree of concentration of ownership. Economic history, therefore, could avoid hard choices between the market and the managed economy, and on the whole, with the brilliant exceptions of Schumpeter, Sombart, and Tawney, it has said surprisingly little about modern capitalism, the agency that has prevailed where all others have failed. Its spirit in relation to its own age has been 'Watch the wall, my darling, while the Gentlemen go by.'

The speed with which economic history put down roots still seems surprising. In the 1870s, not a dog barked; the subject (outside Germany) hardly had a name. Yet by 1892, the first chair in the subject existed. It had an established place in undergraduate teaching for the new history degrees. It had its new and weighty general textbooks, Cunningham's *Growth of English History and Commerce* (1882) and Ashley's *Introduction to Economic History*. It was perhaps at most one generation behind the new constitutional history of Stubbs, then still only entering upon its phenomenally successful claim to be history in general. By the end of the 1880s, economic history was fully conscious of itself as such (unlike the motley crew of previous writers who had written economic history without being conscious of, or assertive about, so doing).

Because economic history was a new endeavour, it offered unusual scope for those outside the narrow world from which academic leaders then normally came. W.J. Ashley (1860-1927), the first holder of a chair in the subject, was the son of a journeyman hatter in Bermondsey; he took a First at Balliol, studied in Germany, and held chairs successively at Harvard and Birmingham. George Unwin, the eldest of six children, was the son of a Stockport railway clerk; leaving school at 13, he took a First at Oxford, and was the first holder of the Manchester chair. William Cunningham (1849-1919) read philosophy at Cambridge (coming joint first in his year with Maitland, the great historian of medieval law). He became an Anglican clergyman, the last such to be a university historian of note, and his final berth was as Archdeacon of Ely.

Academic socialism was represented by Toynbee, the Webbs, and Tawney. Arnold Toynbee (1852-83), an Oxford scholar whose *The Industrial Revolution* (1882) coined a phrase not hitherto used in English, was perhaps the first of the line (not counting Marx if only because he was a German writing in German for Germans). R.H. Tawney, a High Church Anglican, extra-mural teacher, and adviser to the Labour party, was academically the most persuasive of the group. The protectionists, sometimes in direct contact, from 1903, with Joseph Chamberlain's Tariff Reform crusade, found institutional support both at Chamberlain's Birmingham University and in the London School of Economics (founded 1895).

All these were involved in the world around them in a way going beyond their normal academic duties. Cunningham – Archdeacon Cunningham, to give him his due – wrote such works as *Christianity and Social Questions* (1910), *The Case against Free Trade* (1911), *Efficiency in the Church of England* (1912), and *The Rise and Decline of Free Trade* (1904). Ashley (who ended as a knight) wrote on *The Tariff Problem* (1903) and *The Progress of the German Working Classes* (1904). Thorold Rogers (1823-90), a friend of Bright and an Anglican High Churchman, was a Liberal M.P. (1880-86), twice professor of political economy at Oxford (1862-67, 1888-90), and as well producing *Six Centuries of Work and Wages*

(1885), became ordained. Tawney, qualified in the field of Tudor economic history, found himself between the wars regulating some of the greatest British industries such as coal and cotton, while setting forth in *Education: The Socialist Policy*, and in *Equality* (1931), ideals for the age. His most influential book, *Religion and the Rise of Capitalism* (1926) made economic history a vehicle for a discussion of the spirit and culture behind economic phenomena.

Between the wars, economic history came of age, albeit stolidly and without fireworks. It did not dominate the historical agenda. That position was reserved for diplomatic history, for which the 1914-18 War did wonders. For men like Herbert Butterfield and A.J.P. Taylor, nothing could quite equal its claims to attention as the ideal historical training.

At a less exalted level, though, the slump definitively established that economies were problematical and needed study. The bearing of this on the daily bread of economic history – gilds, fulling-mills, and villeinage – was decidedly indirect, and the subject did not become a vehicle for Thirties political radicalism. Instead, economic history thrived institutionally. All undergraduates reading history – then the dominant subject in English universities – had to study economic history; that was a battle the new subject did not have to fight.

A symptom of growing confidence was the foundation of the Economic History Society in 1926. Its membership, by 1975, was about 2,500 (though it has since declined[1] to about 1,750 in 1993). Its journal, the *Economic History Review*, begun the same year, soon acquired a pontifical standing rare among journals, perhaps because the cult of the article (or 'latest article') has played a curiously large part in the growth of the subject. Looking back, it would seem that, for all the heroic labours and outsize personalities of its early days, economic history really did not have to struggle too hard, as new subjects go, to establish itself as a proper part of university history; and that its harder struggle began after 1945, when it sought to tie its fortunes to keeping up with the social sciences.

The institutional and pedagogic context of economic history has

[1] The peak year for A-level entries in economic history (in the UK) was back in 1971. Thereafter it became a magnet for weaker quality candidates, which 'general history' did not.

varied greatly over time, and perhaps even more between place and place; but probably economics has been the main, and increasing, influence. Here economic history perhaps did not fulfil expectations – had not Schmoller expected abstract economics discreetly to wither away as economic history replaced it with reality? Economic history, far from challenging theoretical economics to come off its high horse, has instead usually trod submissively in its master's footsteps. When econometrics came in, much of economic history succumbed to the beauty of numbers, and the lure of the barely calculable. This was especially so in the 1960s, when the prestige of social science combined the authority of science and the novelty of revelation.

Econometrics – quantitative contortions using imperfect data to put forward fairly ordinary opinions – commanded huge rewards, in cash and status, for economists; why be left behind? But the rewards have not accrued, at least to the subject of economic history generally. The process at work led away from the sun; an initial sense of being overshadowed by economics has led to intense specialization and declining intelligibility, leading in turn to increasing marginalization, leading to more sense of being overshadowed.

Econometrics came to be linked, perhaps partly by chance, with the question of the counter-factual: that is, 'what would have happened if ...?' Philosophically, this was new ground. History had hitherto talked of what happened, not of what might have happened. Each historical event was supposedly unique, incomparable, not to be contrasted, as in science, with some control. If anything was gospel, this was. Yet here was W. Fogel answering with formidable rigour what would have happened to the U.S. economy had the railroads not been built. (Answer: less than you might have thought.)

Fogel's very excellence in econometric technique was a distraction from his real achievement. So was the fact that not all users of his method agreed. The not entirely serious name of 'cliometrics' perhaps also threw sand in some eyes. The real interest of Fogel's work was not economic, or statistical, or American, or methodological; it was philosophical. It made the question 'What would have happened if one variable were altered?' a legitimate part of historical discussion. And in doing so, it enlarged the tasks of history in general, not just of history in its economic or numerate varieties; for 'What if?' is philosophically no less legitimate, if perhaps technically more difficult, in any other context. Thanks to a development in economic history, every unique event or process now bore with it counter-factual brethren as part of its uniqueness.

Economic history is a house of many mansions. Business history, certainly one distinct version, with its own distinct history inside the history of economic history, is perhaps still an underdeveloped area, surprisingly so given the amazing global success of corporate capitalism. Even more surprisingly, business history is at its weakest in the study of financial markets – Wall St and the City; these have had few academic friends. Yet despite this sense of working against the grain in this area, economic history has added a word, an idea, and an altered sense of perspective to our common culture, by its coinage of the word 'entrepreneur'. This comes from a book of 1911 by the economic historian Schumpeter, assisted by a long subsequent Harvard institute and chair, and the journal *Explorations in Entrepreneurial History*. The word entered common use, because it seemed important to a very few academics that it should do so; and it was held important by them, because the word was seen (latterly in a Cold War context) as pointing persuasively to an important social truth.

The study of how governments run economies and take economic decisions is by contrast strongly developed. It is here that economic history (being in this branch essentially archival) is least distinguishable from political history generally. Academics, in history as elsewhere, are more drawn to government than to business; irrationally, both subjects being about the relation of people to their contexts, and being about the control of much by the few, in fairly equal degree.

The most empirical school, that represented with conscious intellectual lowliness by Sir John Clapham, was happy to fix its eyes on how men earned their livings, making that their point of departure. In more recent works of grand synthesis, a genre in which the subject is rich, the idea of a description so full that it is also an explanation remains one major form of ambition. Though it is a matter of degree, this gentle reportage is a far cry from economic history in which 'the economy' or 'growth' rules, with empirical detail subservient to unhistorical abstraction (or ungeographical ones, for the economic realities of specific regions, trades, and markets are placed at the mercy of data defined by usually political boundaries).

The tensions between 'bottom up' and 'top down' history exist in economic as in political history, but linked to the tension between empiricism and abstraction. Sometimes indeed 'the economy' becomes a disembodied hero, exogenous even to its own natural components and reacting with them. It becomes a sort of soccer team still breathing the ethos of competitiveness which Victorian historians instilled into political history; and fierce indeed are the statistical rivalries over growth rates as measured by 'my' pair of dates against the other man's. The atmosphere is one almost of sport and of goals scored. So far as economic history is a history of abstractions, it mainly enshrines a postwar religion of 'growth', with all its false hopes and assumptions one of the great twentieth-century fallacies; and thus an area of uncritical belief whose roots need exposing.

Like all the social sciences, economic history faces a stark choice between being narrowly modern in scope, or becoming too inaccurate to support pretensions to a quantitative, theorizing, scientific vocation. Abundance of quantitative data is an essentially modern phenomenon, with the first Census (1801) marking a symbolic division between a dubiously accurate Age of Statistics and a pre-statistical past. But abundance of quantitative data is not the same thing as abundance of accurate data; far from it. In the view of one leading authority, the great majority of historical statistics before the Second World War are too approximate to be suitable material for the application of mathematical methods of any but the most elementary kind. Attempts to treat them in that way can usually be ignored, not only with safety but with advantage. Another professor of economic history is fractionally more generous, urging that good work in quantitative economic history requires a lot of statistical information, and there is seldom enough for almost any decade before 1920.

Even of the authoritative, much-revised, indispensable *British Historical Statistics*[1], it has been noted by a third authority 'that

[1] Ed. B.R. Mitchell. Revised ed., 1988.

virtually all the data in this volume are subject to significant margins of error – some to very wide error, such that they are little more than rough guesses'. When the Holy Writ of the economic historian is so uncertain, the quality of judgments and speculations based on this kind of material hardly bears thinking about. At best, the errors may accidentally cancel out; more probably, they will multiply in number and magnitude when put together in argument. Without statistics by the shovelful, economic history is unthinkable; with them, it is inherently unreliable, above all where the topic is not the particular, but something as general as the inner workings and dynamics of a whole economy. This is not an objection to economic history so much as a reminder that its unlikeness to political history can be exaggerated; both build on frail foundations, both deal in uncertainties.

Where does economic history fit in? For a century its practitioners have not quite known. Some say with history, some with economics, some prefer independence. No final answer is in sight. The most one can say is that from its early days economic history has been more separate from history than any other historical specialism. So far as this stems from the argument that it requires a knowledge of economic theory, it has some rational basis. But this argument, if pressed, would hardly support a case for full independence; yet linkage with economics is perhaps the least generally acceptable solution. And withdrawal into its shell usually means, in practice, withdrawal into an inconveniently small shell. So, again in practice, the debate continues.

Judged by the offshoots it has sprouted, rather than by its own indeterminate status, economic history has proved fertile. There is agricultural history (as at Reading), local history (as at Leicester), and the use of aerial photography. There are M.W. Beresford's lost medieval villages. There is oral history (as at Essex). There is transport history. In uncertain relation, there is social history, in general, which usually hived off from economic history. There is the new biological and ecological history, a mainly American phenomenon designed to make the White Man properly guilt-ridden about the impact of Columbus on native American societies. There is the history of medicine, and of technology. There is population history, one of the greatest academic successes of the last generation – or perhaps one of Henry VIII's great successes, for it was his legislation which provided the parish registers over four centuries on which the new techniques of family reconstitution are based. If the measure of vitality in a subject is its rate of fragmentation, then economic history is a success.

XIII

Modern Schools of History

The simplest thing that can be said about historical writing as the twentieth century ends, is that it remains conspicuously national in character. French, Germans, Americans, English, go their separate ways. (Where is the major book by a Frenchman on Germany, or by a German on France?) This is not to deny some flow of influence, chiefly from French social history and American social science; but what they seek to modify is one or other national base. Conversely, the type of history that has not emerged anywhere is world history, the history of man upon earth as preached so eloquently and to such a vast public by H.G. Wells in the 1920s. That is undoubtedly a disappointment.

There are world histories, and good ones, like J.M. Roberts's *Penguin History of the World*, but they are more the sum of the various professional regional histories, than a cultural new departure. If world history ever does come, its most likely point of departure will be an ecological or 'Green' history which already speaks to all mankind.

World history, then, is the thing that is most obviously missing as the century ends; and one reason for this is that even where innovation is most consciously novel, as in France and America, it is reluctant to move far beyond its national boundaries. Another reason is linguistic. History follows the flag, or perhaps the tongue, with Africa and Latin America historically colonized in a way that linguistically more resistant Asia was not. Islam remains the last historical frontier for Europeans: one where cultural patronage avails nothing.

Let us look at the state of historical understanding as it will be in the early parts of the next century. In terms of areas studied, we shall perhaps have done the right thing for the wrong reasons. African history, once undertaken because emotionally it was 'ours', will be inescapably important; it will be the history of the nearly one-third of humanity soon to be born as Africans. Latin American history, once a thriving soft option covering a torpid backwater, has become that of a continent at last enjoying a long predicted awakening. Post-Cold War Europe has regained an identity and cohesion which means that those whose teaching and research reflected the world as it was before 1914, now find that their very failure to modernize has made them suddenly appropriate. The history of the United States, existing earlier this century primarily because it mattered to Americans, has become supremely important to non-Americans. Though perhaps economically outstripped, and militarily anachronistic, America, as the only cultural superpower, is central to the world history of next century. Thus it would seem as we look ahead that all is for the best, as we consider how our historical insight is matched to what will shortly need to be understood. Alas, such optimism is only a way of saying that we do not understand Asia and will not need to: a world of Africa, Europe, and the Americas represents perhaps the natural limit beyond which historical understanding will not easily stretch. Since historians, like doctors, take decades rather than years to manufacture and deploy, misjudgment about the Asian 'trimmings' will prove hard to rectify.

Most late Victorian developments have endured. The rooting of historical practice within national cultures, the lack of a trend towards world history, the establishment of a historical profession and its location within universities, the corresponding marginalization of popular and literary history, are all much in 2000 as in 1900, and are unlikely to change. Subject to that overall unity, however, one can divide the age of English professional history into two periods, the first that of the medieval supremacy, the second that of fragmentation, with the break coming about 1950 or 1960.

Medieval constitutional history, until about 1950, was the touchstone against which the rest of historical scholarship was measured. There were good reasons for this. It was beyond doubt technically advanced. It had its own inner law of progress, as it moved from rich chronicle to uniquely rewarding public records, playing off one against the other. It sought to explain what mattered most – parliament and law. Its use of primary sources offered an exacting training to students.

But there were cracks in the edifice. Medieval history, restless minds said, was not modern. Its concern with parliament and law had dated badly. It was far from politically realistic. It had pursued legalisms beyond what was profitable. Its rigorous use of mainly Latin sources had simply become impractical as the teaching of Latin receded in the schools. The most telling charge was the one least made: that medieval constitutional history undervalued or omitted huge areas of what was most important in medieval civilization. Taken together, there was enough truth in all this to give an inevitable piecemeal victory to those who cried change; but their victory consisted more in movement away from the existing state of things, than towards any well-defined goal. A break occurred about 1950 or 1960, and medieval studies passed from the role of common formative experience, to a ghettoized historical subculture for enthusiasts, with its own internal lines of fragmentation.

Of the two lines of development which twentieth-century history might have taken, towards universal or world history, and towards history as argument about evidence, it is the latter which has done better, particularly in the teaching of history in schools. If lip service were all that were required, history from evidence would command the field. The reality is that the going of medieval history marked a decisive setback to a tradition of evidence-based historical analysis as a way of teaching long periods of history. Stubbs' *Select Charters* moved in a few years about 1950 from centrality to oblivion. At student level, the tradition of rigorous study of a tightly defined body of evidence, has been replaced by opinions about opinions.

Modern diplomatic history might have come to fill the dominant position vacated by a receding medievalism. Had that gap occurred in the 1930s, instead of after 1945, diplomatic history probably would have inherited its mantle as the main form of rigorous historical training. As it is, it has come near to fading out. Part of the reason relates to differing perceptions of the two World Wars.

The First War made diplomatic history look crucial. The Second World War made it seem unnecessary. Diplomatic history, it was hoped, could trace the origins of the 1914 war, and settle the contentious issue of war guilt. It might even pronounce on whether the Great War had been a mistake. No issues could be more important; and diplomatic history prospered accordingly. After 1945, the consensus that the Second War was caused by Hitler (and that was that – no problematic origins, no problematic culpability, no uncertainty as to its necessity) made 'what one clerk wrote to another clerk', the whole business of diplomatic action, a ridiculous superficiality which answered none of the real questions. The almost complete decline of diplomatic history since 1945 is a classic instance, not only of soft options driving out hard ones, but of the way changes in non-academic opinion about which questions really matter can define the work expected of an academic subject.

Because twentieth-century history is first and foremost a profession, it produces almost by definition wave upon wave of eminent, worthy, actively successful professional men. In that sense, history has been successful indeed – that is as a profession. In 1970, responses to an American Historical Association questionnaire showed that of its 13,000 members, 92% were full-time professional historians. The number of leading figures really is very large, the advances in knowledge made very considerable. To notice each and every one would be impossibly lengthy, to confine oneself arbitrarily to some and omit others would be unfair. But this is no barren stock: the hopes of the Victorian founding fathers have been amply fulfilled, and a rich body of evidence has yielded a rich harvest. Professional history in the twentieth century has been immensely productive. For British historians, however, there was one notable loss, and perhaps one that would matter more than anything in the long run: the loss of standing, if not of esteem, in the American educational world, where by 1970 only 4% of historians taught British history.

One has to look for something extra, therefore, before considering naming names: that element of moral or intellectual challenge which comes as a shock. Two names in particular occur. Neither belonged to any school; neither left a school behind him. E.P.

Thompson's *The Making of the English Working Class* (1963) startled by its power of identifying with the victimhood of the poor. It hardly mattered that it could almost serve as an unintended obituary for working-class politics in a suburban nation, that its underdogs are too naively admired, or that its sociology perhaps claimed too much too soon. Its moral challenge was immense.

'Moral challenge' hardly describes A.J.P. Taylor, the historian best known to the post-war public. His speed of mind amounted to genius. As a student of diplomatic documents, as a lecturer on great subjects, as writer of reviews, and as author of works of synthesis, especially *The Struggle for Mastery in Europe* (1954), he could see through a brick wall in four largely unrelated ways. 'All is not what it seems', was his motto. Like Thompson, Taylor was as much outside as inside the main stream of university life. Intellectually, neither man affected historical practice. It is not as innovators, or leaders of a school, that we remember them, but for their individual qualities as remarkable human beings.

Not a person, but a periodical, marked the consensus of the Fifties. *Past and Present*, founded in 1952, marked orthodoxy, not as it was, but as it wished to become. With more than a sprinkling of leading academic Communists on its board, it was accordingly defensive and muted in its political tone, its central message being that the social dimension behind all history was under-explored (as it certainly was). This wish to reinterpret general history in a more social way sharply distinguished it from the social history of the Sixties, an attempt to found one more specialism among many. *Past and Present* stood for life, debate, a new and attractive style. It was there to be admired, and it was admired; yet it was either too catholic or too unaggressive to establish itself as a journal-based ideology like the *Annales* group in France.

The fragmentation of history has reigned without much wish to restrain it since 1950. There were so many reasons for this that it is easy to overlook perhaps the most obvious: that the twentieth century had itself become history. In the United Kingdom, this effect was especially marked, because the Labour government of 1964-70 changed the Fifty Year Rule governing the release of official papers, to a Thirty Year Rule. Thus in 1964, history officially went up to 1914; in 1994, it goes up to 1964. This in turn blurred well-established academic boundaries, especially between History and Politics. The historian could no longer see Politics, as a subject, as 'yesterday's newspapers' or 'history without the evidence', or at least not so easily, for contemporary history of varying degrees of contemporaneity was asserting its rightful place once again to the position it had after all held from Thucydides to Clarendon.

It is only in the last few centuries that the essence of great history has not been its contemporaneity. Within the teaching of modern history itself, a once perhaps just manageable modern period centring on the English or European nineteenth century became an attempt to cope with two centuries, nineteenth and twentieth, without anyone having intended it; and however long delayed, the idea of a post-1789 or post-1832 modern period must fragment under the strain.

Where a general if diffuse counter-tendency has occurred it is in the wish to make obeisance to social history, or even sociology. There are many levels of explanation for this; it is not just a matter of pointing to the great French *Annales* school of social historians. It is an international phenomenon. It looks back with entire logic to the Romantic idea of the nation. It has nineteenth-century forerunners; and twentieth-century practitioners who were more than offshoots of French ideas. G.M. Trevelyan's *Social History of England*, the wartime bestseller, was the best example of social history as the product of the lighter moments of an established political historian. In J.H. Plumb, the movement towards social history, especially of the world of luxury, again came from an established and serious political historian.

Yet what is social history? Ask ten historians, and you will get nine different answers.

One may say: the history of everyday life. This is probably the popular answer. A second may say, the history of the everyday life of the poor (which is not quite the same). A third may say it is the study of dissidence, of the seething resentment beneath the calm surface of social structure, of the storm to be found in every teacup. There is a great tradition here: Hilton, Tawney, Christopher Hill, E.P. Thompson, G. Rudé, R. Cobb, have created a genre of almost formulaic writing in which the peasants are always rising and the toilers always dispossessed – and the distinction between social and political history is more than a little blurred. A fourth may argue that the starting point of social history is the history of public policy for dealing with the unfortunate: social policy, more or less, and not far from being the political (and archival) history of institutions. A fifth may want to look mainly at the changing history of social structure, while a sixth may be concerned with what historical demography can tell us about the nature of the family (and even of sexuality). Others may define social history in terms of preference for a particular method. They may find revelation in the history of mentalities, or in the quantitative approach – the 'beauty of numbers'; or they may look to the unique character of oral history.

That makes nine, anyway. Social history *is* very divided, very centrifugal. In places it lacks any real dividing line from political history, just as it lacks any real unity, even of method, with economic history, with which it has been institutionally linked on the tenuous grounds that both are relative newcomers. The traditional fondness of social history for the poor, for social policy and social reform, for the history of oppression (politics in masquerade) probably derives more from the political commitments of a previous academic generation than from the essential nature of the subject. The blurred and indefinite character of social history has not stood in the way of good work, and so nobody should sigh over it.

The history of art, though an old subject, may fairly be noticed here, for only in the last generation has it taken its place in the broadening of the contents of higher education. Like most apparent specialisms, and like social history, it turns out on closer inspection to be itself a group of none too firmly related endeavours.

Its profile is distinctive. Its roots go far deeper than the history of music or of science. It sets little store by criticism, certainly compared with literary studies. It moves nimbly if uncertainly between two quite dissimilar bodies of evidence: paintings and documents. It can encase its facts in a broad and sweeping view of history; thus Vasari's *Lives of the Painters* (1551) tells how art improves, step by step, in an evolutionary way, albeit with cyclical overtones. This was Whig history indeed; as Ruskin's *The Stones of Venice,* with its story of moral decline set forth in art, was Whig history in reverse.

Four approaches in particular stand out. One is the attempt, by the German Winckelmann among others, to discern large philosophic ideas behind art, especially the art of antiquity. The second concerns the approach, notably associated with the Swiss Burckhardt, which saw in art material for social and cultural history. The third concerns connoisseurship, or the development of the expertise needed to establish what was painted by whom. Fourthly, and lastly in time, one may name iconography, or the understanding of why the contents of pictures were what they were. From these disparate elements, sometimes mainly one, sometimes another, the art history of today has emerged.

The French 'historical revolution' is perhaps the dominant feature of the twentieth-century historical landscape. Both from inside and outside, it is seen as a movement, with leaders and followers, based on truths and beliefs, shared intimacies, shared student days, great works, manifestos and slogans and sloganizers. But, before we turn to the *Annales* school, to give it its workaday name, one feature of its success needs discussion: the lack of competition from Germany, America, and England.

German historiography, especially since 1945, has been inward-looking, concerning itself above all with the special fate, or '*Sonderweg*' of modern Germany. At its simplest, it asks 'Where did we go wrong?' This could hardly fail to turn on events and politics. Its great works, like Fritz Fischer's *Griff nach der Weltmacht* (1961), published in English as *Germany's Aims in the First World War* (1966), deepened the picture of German guilt in 1914. Instead of war by accident or war by railway timetable, it substituted a picture of war by deliberate German decision and desire. This represented not only the triumph of deep research, but the triumph of a younger academic generation over the older conservative nationalism of the German post-war historical establishment. Discussion of Fischer's theme was very much on party lines; Fischer's new orthodoxy came to look distinctly Social Democratic. It was a great advance in knowledge, one that was very widely accepted; there was no reason why it could not have been made by Frenchmen, or Americans, or Englishmen.

But French history did not cross the Rhine, even for something so important as establishing why war broke out in 1914. French history, while benefiting greatly from lack of ideological competition from abroad, won its spurs by seeming not to notice the great events of its own century.

American cultural dominance has affected historiography less than almost any other area of literature. Americans dominate the study of the United States (and probably of Latin America, and perhaps of Asia in European languages): nothing else. Americans produced their nineteenth-century classics of literary history in the New England school of Parkman (1823-93), Motley (1814-77) and Prescott (1796-1859) – all Harvard men. If they now seem remote, it is not from any inherent lack of merit, nor because their part in the localized flowering of high culture in Boston, Massachusetts was not as remarkable as it was precocious but because they suffered from the general supersession of literary history. These writers come at the last stage of a European tradition which they could do little to modify. Bancroft (1800-1891), less literary and more of a toiler, more resembled the seventeenth-century seekers after original sources; he studied at a German university when few did so, and he published in twelve volumes a minutely thorough account of the origins of the United States (1834-1882) based on the original documents. The United States began its career as a producer of history with a slight lead over Europe which it has perhaps never lost. With the decline of literary history as conceived by America's Victorians, their successors Turner and Beard presented an intellectual challenge but one which to the non-American lacks general interest. Who, outside America, cared if the constitution was not all that Americans thought?

Not the French of the *Annales* school. They no more crossed the Atlantic than they crossed the Channel or the Rhine. *Annales*, the journal, was founded in 1929 to promote a new kind of history, rather than to extend its scope.

The French revolution in history was associated with the journal *Annales* (its titles and subtitles have varied), founded in 1929. But it is a mistake to place too much stress on the journal itself as a mouthpiece for new points of view. The *Annales* movement was something wider – a circle, a club, a conspiracy, a cult, above all a power base. Its ideas were not all that unusual in any country at the time: the unusual feature was the way they endured and turned into a historical regime which did not exist in other countries. This is what is special about the French school: its continuity and its centralization, so that one can speak of a single historical heritage over perhaps sixty years.

It is easier to define *Annales* by what it rejected than by what it proclaimed. It rejected the narrative history of states, of politics, and events; the biographies of monarchs, the 'drums and trumpets' of battles, and the skilled drudgery of diplomatic history. Instead, it sought the history of society, of all of society, 'total history'. In terms of method, it sought to be inter-disciplinary, bringing together history, geography, economics, psychology, and anthropology. In terms of space, it sought to expand the limits of history beyond the restrictions of periodization and particular land masses or oceans. It was not necessarily 'history from below', though it often came to be so, especially in its intensive regional studies. It was not on the whole politically oriented or motivated, though Marxism entered in later on when it entered everything. It was intensely French; its main works were rarely translated until the 1970s and its masterpiece, Braudel's *Méditerranée*, was not reviewed in the English historical press when it came out.

It served people interested in French identity and French social history supremely well. Though campaigning against limitations, it was mainly early modern history, and secondarily medieval history that concerned it. It produced little on the nineteenth, and nothing on the twentieth century, and left Germany and the United States well alone. As such, it became a vehicle of French cultural and intellectual supremacy, well worthy of the government backing that it obtained after the war. The message that benighted foreigners were meant to receive was that the French knew more about the history of French society than any other country knew about theirs. This was indeed perhaps so though there was a simple reason for French historians' involvement with the peasantry. It was the guillotine, which had abruptly precluded the study of a landowning class identified with the conduct of national business and ready, as in Britain, to welcome academic inquiries.

Annales was the creation of two men, Marc Bloch, shot by the Germans in 1944, and Lucien Febvre, a man of combative and vehement nature, who died in 1956. Before the war, its achievement was the books of these two men: it was then an influence, but not, probably, the regime that it later became. However, it sincerely believed in a 'new history' and put its beliefs into practice, the more so since the two men worked together at Strasbourg in the 1920s. Bloch's main works were *The Royal Touch, French Rural History* (1931), *Feudal Society* (1939-40), Bloch's main work, which deals with the cultural history of feudalism, not just its material side, *Strange Defeat* (1946), a war book, *The Historian's Craft* (1949), this last not the work of an iconoclast or ideologue as might be expected. Of these, *The Royal Touch* was the single most important work.

Febvre's field was the Renaissance and Reformation in France: his best-known work *The Problem of Unbelief in the Sixteenth Century*, which looked forward to post-war work in the history of mentalities – what it was possible to think at a given time. After the war, Febvre was in power; became more a man of power than a prolific writer. It was his post-war role as state historian that made his pre-war role so significant. His temperament well fitted him to lead a semi-official reorganization of learning, as president of the Sixth Section (founded 1947) of the École Pratique des Hautes Études, and director of the Centre des Recherches Historiques until his death in 1956. In a country with an educational system as centralized as that of France, the personality and views of the man at the top mattered enormously. Febvre created an empire; Fernand Braudel inherited and expanded it, until he in turn died in 1985.

Already by Febvre's death the *Annales* movement embodied many strands. At its simplest, it was the views and influence of a leading periodical and its editors. Going back to student days, it asserted a general opposition to the history of politics and events, and a support for problem-based history, which was not uncommon among early twentieth-century critics of the historical establishment in all countries.

Another element was a belief in the need for an inter-disciplinary approach. This reflected as much as anything the simple fact that Bloch and Febvre, having both received the highly interdisciplinary education offered by the École Normale Supérieure, continued to propound the collegiate values they had imbibed in that hothouse, and developed when together in an intense academic circle at Strasbourg in the 1920s.

But the reason it did not stop there, as an interesting tendency in medieval and early modern social history, lay essentially in the scope created by the post-war educational reconstruction in France for some pre-war senior academic figure to turn ideology into institutional power. Where *Annales* differed from other movements for historical revival lay in its having the power and authority to do the things it wanted to do, and for that a world war was needful. By the 1950s *Annales* was the historical establishment in France, and it put its position to good use.

Fernand Braudel was Lucien Febvre's chosen 'son' and successor in a movement based throughout on close personal ties. Until his death in 1985, Braudel was the leading French historian, perhaps (if the slot existed) the leading European historian, and his work *La Méditerranée* (1949) was the model for the new history in its middle phase – that is, before the arrival of quantitative history (or the 'poetry of numbers') and the history of mentalities created a third avant-garde wave.

Braudel was the French historical establishment, a new establishment still enjoying a reputation for radicalism and rebellion, which in Braudel's case took the form of an intense attachment to historical geography or 'geohistory' on a vast scale. Braudel's career was unusual by the standards of Anglo-Saxon (or German) academic normality.

Born in 1902 Braudel studied at the Sorbonne, spent ten years as a schoolmaster in Algeria (1923-32), two years teaching at the University of San Paulo (1935-7), was a prisoner-of-war in Germany during the Second War, and was awarded his doctorate, begun in the 1920s, in 1947. This became a book of 600,000 words, *The Mediterranean*, in 1949, when he was in his later forties: it was his first important publication. It transformed French history, though its subject matter was not specifically French. In its vastness, and the sense it conveyed of individual insignificance, it has been compared to Tolstoy's *War and Peace*. At any rate, it was the masterpiece the *Annales* movement sought, and it embodied, in its three parts, a conception of total history in which environmental change played a fundamental and irresistible part.

Braudel was perhaps best summed up as geographical determinism plus poetry: he wrote memorably of how men are 'crushed' by 'the huge weight of distant origins'. Yet neither quantitative history, nor the history of mentalities, nor political leftism, was part of his formula. There was a further revolution to come before *Annales* took the even more memorable form it takes today. All the while, lesser but still very considerable figures were at work on exhaustive studies of provincial France, raising the regional monograph to new levels.

It was Ernest Labrousse, a Marxist and a figure rather apart from the rest, who was 'the father of the movement towards quantitative history in France' in the period from the 1950s to the 1970s, when it becomes probably the best-known feature of *Annales* history, so well-known that the phrase 'the beauty of numbers' began to circulate. Labrousse reintroduced events into the centre of *Annales* history by offering numerically based explanations of the biggest event of all: the French Revolution. His *Sketch of the Movement of Prices and Revenues in 18th-Century France* (1933) dealt with prices 1701-1817; leading up to *The Crisis of the French Economy* (1944) which emphasized the economic crisis of the late 1780s as a precondition of the Revolution.

One can hardly not mention here the longest thesis ever written, Pierre and Huguette Chaunu's *Seville and the Atlantic* (1955-60: 12 vols.) with vol. 8, on interpretation, running to 3,000 pages of text, which used Braudel's method and Spanish overseas trade figures to write the history of the Atlantic in terms of an enormous time series.

Braudel's empire gradually fragmented with the passage of time. *Annales*, the journal, passed into younger hands, while in 1972 Braudel retired from the presidency of the Sixth Section, which disappeared in a reorganization in 1975. Braudel had no successor, in the sense of someone able to combine intellectual authority and a unifying administrative position. And yet, writers of very various dispositions and interests continued to see themselves, in this third generation, as members of an *Annales* tradition, and were seen abroad as its spokesmen and leaders. The controversies over the true nature of history remained as fierce as in the days of the founding fathers.

Two developments were specially notable. One came from Philippe Ariès, not himself an academic historian, whose famous *Centuries of Childhood* (1965) and *The Hour of our Death* (1981) continued the tradition of Febvre. The other came from Le Roy Ladurie, the greatest celebrity of the last generation of French historians, partly because of his authorship of the best-selling *Montaillou* (1978), a work which perhaps owed more to the painstaking methods of the Inquisition, and partly because he was a pugnacious controversialist on matters at large, as in *The Territory of the Historian* (1979), and a prolific writer on French social history. To him, the *Annales* movement was still a creed, a matter of separating sheep and goats, a view widely accepted as the hallmark of historical authenticity around the world.

This was at least a little odd. *Annales* history was as narrowly French as German history was narrowly German. *Annales* history simply did not adapt to the study of the nineteenth and twentieth centuries. These were formidable limitations. Perhaps the *Annales* movement, like French cuisine and French haute couture, was an exercise in public relations, backed ultimately by governmental money and power. Was there an underlying unity, other than mutual personal approval, in this succession of methodological innovations? It is rather extraordinary that the initial, not very original rejection of political narrative should suffice for almost a century as a platform for unifying French historical entrepreneurship in all its varied forms.

Postscript

A Year On

Behind every book there lies a tale. This one is no exception. It began, long ago, when as a newcomer to Bristol I was asked to devise a freshman course on history. Devise I duly did, with assistance from a folder containing the efforts of other universities in this direction. No history department had found the study of history altogether easy going; the Sixties, then just passed, might tug one way, towards more conceptual approaches to history but historians themselves, young and old, were never ones for concepts, let alone for rigour. The wind of 'reform', as academic restlessness is called, blew this way and that down ensuing decades. Sometimes the Study of History was on the Bristol menu, sometimes it was off. Each time my folders grew a little larger. At any rate, nobody took much notice of what was said: a most satisfactory state of affairs. I began even to imagine that I represented some kind of consensus about the nature and history of history.

Foolish thoughts, no doubt. Yet behind them lay a reason of sorts – the curious pre-eminence in this particular field of one single text, E.H. Carr's Penguin on *What is History?*, a text which by combining chattiness, Leftishness, lack of rigour, and thorough scepticism, seemed everywhere to lend academic legitimacy to Study of History courses. (A parallel perhaps was Bernard Crick's *In Defence of Politics*, another Penguin, which had an important role in underpinning the legitimacy of politics as a new-born subject.) Crick, indeed, had sold 500,000 copies: temptation surely – and as for Carr, surely his insights, derived largely from diplomatic history, would not be seen as the full story forever? Such thoughts crossed my mind but not until I received an invitation from Oxford University Press to write on the subject did the ambition to write take active form.

Since OUP and I eventually fell out, all too publicly, over this book, it is important to make clear that it was not always so. True, there was no contract, only an invitation. I took OUP on trust, which, as the press later pointed out, was a great mistake on my part. However, I had reason. My draft was read once by Oxford, and praised; a second time, to their broad satisfaction. Since the second reader was Sir Keith Thomas, President of the British Academy, whose word counts for much with the Press, matters seemed promising. Throughout a summer the publisher urged me to make haste; set a date for publication; entered on the question of the appearance of the cover. If it was not marriage, at least the date of the nuptials was settled, and we had moved to discuss the colour of the gowns.

Then enthusiasm as suddenly gave way to lack of enthusiasm. A third reader, chosen by Sir Keith Thomas, appeared on the scene. His or her report – the identity was never rumbled, though the commitments were clear – was leaden: the third reader was as present-centred as my text was past-centred. He, or she, thought the current generation of historians were the people who mattered; and I did not. A difference of opinion, perhaps, but OUP frowned on such differences of opinion, even if done at its invitation and with its previously expressed approval. Moreover, other matters surfaced, though they came to be given an undue importance in press reports. Thus the Oxford reader decried the absence of politically correct language (though OUP claims not to insist on this) and the absence of any tribute to Sir Keith Thomas's great book. That absence I gladly remedy now.

Anyway, it was an open-and-shut rejection from that point on, with no chance given to modify the book in the light of the reader's comments, and the matter indeed never got as far as the Delegates, or governing body, of the Press. (What do the Delegates do, if not decide on publication in the light of readers' reports?) The door having been banged shut, by the very editor who had spent the previous summer urging haste, that was that, and I did not expect this book ever to be published.

Improbably, and fully four months after rejection, the higher journalism got wind of the episode. The Thames, much to my surprise, caught fire; parts of the OUP reader's report, such as its suggestion that politically correct feminist language be used, did indeed give hostages to fortune. The Telegraph railed; The Times fumed. My case was even discussed, in absentia of course, on the Melvyn Bragg show. The university authorities in their wisdom set out to prevent me from communicating with the media or broadcasting on a BBC history magazine programme of unsurpassed inoffensiveness and innocence. Such is fame, or the illusion of it, and it is exceedingly momentary. At the end of it all, however, this book was as far from being rescued from oblivion as ever.

Then came the happy ending; I found my white knight in Duckworth, or rather they found me, and I take this opportunity to thank them. Born of Bloomsbury, Duckworth has been innovative, liberal-minded, not tied to conventional opinion as a huge university press like OUP, tied to the American market, perhaps has to be; and if Duckworth does not enforce the modern academic narrowness, it could be because it's unusually well ahead of it.

It was only later that I learned that OUP had been the subject of a judicial rebuke for their commercial ethics in the matter of contracts. Rejected authors should be quite clear that the law will sometimes uphold their case, whether contract has been signed or not – a point of no little interest, and as little known.

Enough about the book's history.

More to the point in this postscript to the new edition, was the reaction of the critics. They spoke with two voices. The second voice, however, was almost mute compared with the first. Almost the sole point selected for public discussion was social history. To the media, from Australia to America, this was the book that had expressed doubt about social history. No matter that I had also expressed vicious doubts about causality, taken a swipe at values, or taken a tough line on bias: nobody wanted to know about such things. Not a squeak came back to me, in fact, on the philosophy of history side. The history of history side was almost equally silent – social history alone excepted (on which there were few enough pages, in all truth). The economic historians, of whom I paint a hardly glowing or cheerful picture, have not come back to me to say

'No, it's not really like that, not as bad as you paint it'. (Perhaps then it *is* as bad as I paint it.) Anyway, by and large I failed hopelessly to stir controversy, whether over economic history or anything else. True, there were objections to my comments on bias; but an objection is not an argument. Worthy folk who spent their working lives teaching that other people had sociologically determined ideas, predictably stood up to testify that they and their friends were not governed by the general rules of sociological influence upon discourse.

But what was it about social history that ruffled so many feathers? There was, after all, no issue in the philosophy of history, or in the history of history, really involved. I say this with full awareness of the looming spectre of post-modernism – though for nearly all purposes, post-modernism and its implications are one thing, and social history and its implications another. Yet the reaction was quasi-religious; had I spoken ill of Proportional Representation, denigrated the Queen Mother, or worn a hat in church, I could not have found myself face to face with a more accusing consensus. I had blasphemed that which was meet to be revered. Underneath, there were questions of curriculum, but these were the least of it: nobody wanted to exhume those pedagogic questions of the '80s. Whatever it was that made social history such a burning issue to so many, it was no longer old-hat anti-Thatcherism.

To an academic teacher, the pattern was familiar. Social history was perceived by students, no doubt wrongly, as an easy option. The lower down the hierarchies of the university system you went, the more they were attuned to social history. The phenomenon was international. Forlornly lost European or American students, victims of a mindless belief in exchange, would come to life at the possibility of studying social history. Why they accepted it, they knew as little as why they rejected the alternatives – but they were programmed, and from an early stage, to believe that here was a straw to be clutched at.

Dim people from dim schools who hoped only to pass unnoticed for three years arrived at university already knowing that their preferences, nay salvation, lay in social history: not economic, and not political. Whereas bright people from good schools, allowed in despite the quota, found no difficulty in a general history that might at times be mostly sharply political while at other times being, as it should be, strongly social. (There is a curious and quite unjustifiable exception made by those who speak in the name of true inclusiveness, or total history: they are apt to exclude, without discussion, the economic dimension, that is, economic history.)

But there is more to social history than being a soft option. Social history is seen as offering or embodying hope – hope of changing society, hope of understanding with finality how the social mechanism actually works, hope of imprinting late twenti-eth-century progressivism upon the world. Political history is not full of comparable hopes. Social history, too, has become dread-fully, interminably, sometimes comically, mixed up with the arrival of gender on the historical scene. On the gender issue above all it is hard to say where widened awareness stops, and the misuse of history for propaganda begins. Any publisher's list, any learned journal, any conference proceedings, anywhere, now re-flects the political agenda of the same global liberal consensus; as why should it not? some will say. And indeed, it may be hard to oppose the newest ways in which truth is made subservient to a political agenda, without falling into the same distortion oneself.

The new narrowness attaches little importance to the whole range of profound issues associated with the philosophy of history. Questions such as causality will not melt away in the face of glib taunts about 'kings and battles'. Yet the part played in historical education today by philosophical topics is slight. Here, surely, there should be more controversy, not less.

Where the history of historical writing is concerned, one may also find grounds for not giving a predominant or exclusive role to social history. For the English historical achievement, over a period of centuries, has been to write the history, not of England alone, but also of antiquity and foreign countries, in ways which have to be explained in terms of English political history. In this view of things, it is English political history which engenders English historical writing: a form of the primacy of the political too complex to explore much in a work of this length.

There is only limited space for argument about what history and historical education can, should, and must consist of. The consensus is strong in favour of total history built around three main pillars which are unlikely to change much. One is political history or the history of power. Another is economic history provided its tendency to separatism can be kept within bounds. A third is the history of thought, including intellectual and cultural history and the history of belief and religion in a broad non-ecclesiastical sense. Those are the pillars. All involve elements of social history, but social history as it now stands is not of itself a pillar, and any claims on its part to an exclusive or predominant role would be quite unjustified. That said, the various contending specialisms which make up social history without doubt have their own place in the scheme of things, but not, for the conceivable future, anything much more.

Further Reading

Peter Burke, *The French Historical Revolution: The Annales School, 1929-89* (1990).

H. Butterfield, *The Whig Interpretation of History* (1931).

E.H. Carr, *What Is History?* (1961).

D.C. Coleman, *History and the Economic Past: an account of the rise and decline of economic history in Britain* (1987).

R.G. Collingwood, *The Idea of History* (1946).

B. Croce, *History Subsumed under the General Concept of Art* (1896).

G. Elton, *The Practice of History* (1967).

G. Elton, *Political History: principles and practice* (1970).

R.W. Fogel and G. Elton, *Which Road to the Past? Two Views of History* (1983).

P. Geyl, *Debates with Historians* (1970).

G.P. Gooch, *History and Historians in the Nineteenth Century* (1913).

N.B. Hart (ed. and introd.) *The Study of Economic History: collected inaugural lectures 1893-1970* (1971).

J.H. Hexter, *Reappraisals in History* (1961).

J.H. Hexter, *Doing History* (1971).

J.P. Kenyon, *The History Men: the historical profession in England since the Renaissance* (1983).

E. Le Roy Ladurie, *The Territory of the Historian* (1979).

E. Le Roy Ladurie, *The Mind and Method of the Historian* (1981).

A. Momigliano, *Studies in Historiography* (1966).

A. Prost, 'What happened to French social history?' *Historical Journal*, xxxv (1992), 671-9.

Raphael Samuel, *Theatres of Memory. Volume One: Past and Present in Contemporary Culture* (1994).

H. Tulloch, *Acton* (1988).

Peter Winch, *The Idea of a Social Science and its Relation to Philosophy* (1958).

Index

academic history, 57-8, 86-90
  economic 93, 95-7
Acton, Lord, 58, 90-1
Africa
  moral judgement on South Africa, 32
  place in world history, 103-4
America
  history in, 111
  place in world history, 103-4
Annales movement, 111-15
Anti-Corn Law League, evidence
  about, 12
Antiquarian Society, 82
Antiquities of Warwickshire
  (Dugdale), 82, 84
archaeology, 4, 81
archives, 9-11, 86
Ariès, Philippe, 116
art history, 109-10
Ashley, W. J., 93, 96
Ashton, T. S., 95
Asia, excluded, 103, 104

Bancroft, G., 111
Baronage (Dugdale), 84
Beard, C. A., 111
Bede, 78
Ben Gurion, David, 64
Beresford, M. W., 101
bias, 51-5
Bible, 6
Bloch, Marc, 113
Bloomsbury group, 58
Bodley, Thomas, 83
Bragg, Melvyn, 119
Braudel, Fernand, 113, 114-15
Bristol University, 117
Britannia (Camden), 81, 82
British Cabinet Ministers 1900-1951,
  13

British Historical Statistics (ed.
  Mitchell), 100-1
Burckhardt, J. C., 110
business history, 99
Butterfield, Herbert, 9, 58-62, 97

Cambridge Modern History (Acton),
  58, 90-1
Camden, William, 81, 82
Camden Society, 87
capitalism, 95
Carlyle, Thomas, 35
Carr, E.H., 117
Catholicism, 63, 83
causality, 46-9
Chamberlain, Joseph, 96
Chartists, evidence about, 12
Christianity
  Butterfield's use of, 61-2
  and Roman Empire evidence, 6
Christianity and History
  (Butterfield), 60, 61-2
*Civilization of the Renaissance in
  Italy, The: An Essay* (Burckhardt),
  35
Clapham, John, 99
class conflict, 72-3
collectors, 82-3
Collingwood, R. G., 21-2, 23-8
Complete Peerage (Cockayne), 84
Conrad, Joseph, 64
conscientious magistrates, 13
conseqences, and morality, 30-1
*Constitutional History of England in
  its Origins and Development, The*
  (Stubbs), 58, 88
constitutionalism, 70
Cotton, Robert, 82-3
counter-factual study, 47-8, 98-9
Cranmer, Thomas, 13